MW01061485

Cole...
I Love You to the
Moon and Back

*A family's
journey with
childhood cancer*

Aaron Dean Ruotsala

Cole...
I Love You to the
Moon and Back

**A family's
journey with
childhood cancer**

*Remembering to live a little brighter,
hug a little tighter, and
love a little longer.*

Aaron Dean Ruotsala

Acknowledgments

I wanted to wait until this book was published to say THANK YOU to all of the thousands of people that literally were our lifeline during this entire episode. In eight short weeks we lost our son but gained an entire new world, a world of knowing who and what the true body of Christ is. We now realize more fully how insignificant the four walls of a physical church building can be. It's the relationships within the body of Christ that matter.

A special thanks go to the following:

The creators of the CaringBridge website. It was this site that helped us get through each day's events. It was a place of comfort and strength and a place where it felt that no matter what condition Cole was in, we always had someone with whom we could talk.

To my beautiful wife, Moireen, who has been my help-mate no matter what the situation has been.

To my cousin, Julie Stenersen, for creating Cole's CaringBridge website and for her undying support during this sad time: www.caringbridge.org/visit/coleruotsala.

To the editors, Alvar Helmes and Carmelle Helmes, who provided invaluable editorial service and suggestions during the writing of this book, and to Stella Wilson and Jane Hannu, who assisted them in this process.

To my children, Chaneille and Whitney – please know that your brother was so brave and strong. May you always know how much he loved you.

Once again, a huge Thank You goes to the entire body of Christ that came together to support and pray for Cole and our entire family during this time.

Contents

Prologue

*L*ike most parents, the thought of having to bury your
child never crossed our minds, especially from a cancer
we had never heard about. Before July 2008, I didn't know
that a cancer like adrenocortical carcinoma even existed.
To think that someone so innocent and who had so much life
ahead of him could even get cancer was beyond our compre-
hension. The topic of "childhood cancer" was completely
unknown to us. Now here I am writing the obituary for my
son Cole. He was the boy who taught us so much. He was the
boy who had over 600,000 hits on his CaringBridge website
in only 2 1/2 months, which averages seven hits per minute,
24 hours a day, for over 60 days. Cole was a boy who has
helped to spread the word about childhood cancer in more
ways than one.

This is a time that helps us realize how little we know
about the future. Our dreams for Cole had everything to do
with the future and who or what he might become. All we
can do now is live with his memories. How precious Cole
was to so many. He was the little boy who always loved to
be by our side no matter what we were doing, the boy who
would wipe away our tears when Mom and Dad wept, the
boy who seemed like he was always teaching us a lesson
instead of us doing the teaching. He was the boy who loved
his younger sister, Chaneille, beyond words, and the boy

who would never forget to pray for our neighbor or anyone else who was on his tender heart at bedtime. He was the boy who made us all remember to hug a little tighter, love a little longer, and always thank God for the gifts He has given. He was COLE!

I am 24 years old and my life was transformed through the life of my son. Shortly after his third birthday, Cole was diagnosed with adrenocortical carcinoma. Within eight short weeks, tumors had grown to encompass both of his lungs, literally cutting off the oxygen and room to breathe. He also underwent an eighteen-hour surgery to remove a tumor from his abdomen that had grown in four short weeks to the point where it filled a one-gallon ice cream bucket.

Cole's illness showed me that God's leading and guiding hand was in the middle of this event from the beginning. My soul was brought to a point that was at its lowest level, and I realized how shallow my life had been. When Cole was lying on his deathbed, it brought me to grips with reality, and I realized what really matters in life. I also realized how very important my role as a father was to my children and how important relationships between people are in this life.

Why did it happen to us? Why Cole, of all people? The questions raced through my mind and my emotions ran wild. The plans for our lives, which were so strategically thought out, were suddenly destroyed to a point where it helped me realize Who really is in control of our lives. I thought I was on top of the world and in control of my destiny, but God had other plans.

"I Love You to the Moon and Back" is a simple phrase that my son told us several times while he was in the hospital. Oh, how he loved us "to the moon and back" – a love that was so innocent and so true, a love that didn't stop at one place but made a full circle. His love was there to show us how our "Father's love" was so great that He sent His Son,

Jesus, to suffer and die that we may live and have life more abundantly.

– Aaron Dean Ruotsala

*C*ole – A little boy whom I never met, yet who touched my heart, along with the hearts of thousands of others around the globe. A little boy, who in eight short weeks, brought all of us together in the common bond of prayer.

Cole – *A little boy who embodied the words of Jesus, our Savior, when He said, "...suffer the little children to come unto Me, for of such is the kingdom of heaven." A little boy who taught us all what childlike faith looks like.*

Cole – *A little boy who showed us the meaning of courage, of trust, of hope – and most of all, who showed us, "...the greatest of these is love."*

Cole – *A little boy who never realized the impact of his short life here on earth, but whose life forever changed us and challenged us to "hug a little tighter, love a little longer." How did a little boy teach us so much?*

Cole – *He did!*

– Carmelle Helmes (co-editor)

My life is forever changed by a little boy named Cole. Although I never met him, I know of him through the CaringBridge website. Cole's journey has brought me closer to my children: I hold them a little tighter and appreciate the "small stuff" more. More importantly, Cole brought me closer to God... for that I am eternally grateful.

– A CaringBridge reader

Chapter 1

Events Prior to Cole's Illness

June 20, 2008, was the day from which all of my thoughts over the next three-month time period originated. This was the day we celebrated Cole's last birthday, a few days earlier than the actual date. This is the story that some would call a nightmare, and the birthplace of what I would call a life-changing experience for myself and thousands of others.

All the signs of a typical birthday party were in place. The invitations had been sent to family and neighbors, and my wife, Moireen, had spent the previous night preparing a sailboat cake for Cole. I was disregarding most of the excitement so I could concentrate on work and what was going on at my job site. I had arrived home later than the time

Moireen and I had agreed upon (typical). I quickly showered and got ready to welcome the guests. The party was already underway, and it wasn't long before the food was ready, the cake was on the table, and the birthday song was being sung for Cole.

Like most birthday parties for three-year-old children, it was more of a social gathering for the adults than anything. While we were visiting, the kids disappeared into the backyard as fast as Cole had slipped under the table when we began to sing to him. They were busy playing and chasing each other around while Cole happened to be pushing a Tonka toy. It was a metal dozer that had an adjustable blade on the front. He was running across the yard when the blade dropped off, and the dozer came to a sudden stop. Unfortunately, Cole didn't stop as fast as the dozer did, and his body was thrown against the metal toy.

Suddenly we were silenced by Cole's scream. It was Mom and Dad to the rescue, as usual. Most times when children get hurt, there isn't much that a kiss on the "owie" or a hug can't cure. However, this one was oddly different. The cries didn't stop any time soon, nor did the swelling that occurred in his abdomen as a result of the accident. It was hard to the touch, so we thought it would be best to take him to the emergency room. We were released from the hospital 3 1/2 hours later with a diagnosis of a severe blow to the abdomen. The x-rays and scans showed no signs of tumors. We went home and things appeared to be normal for Cole the following day.

Most summers seem to go by faster and faster every year that goes by. This particular summer was no different. Every weekend was completely booked from July to September. After Cole's birthday incident, life went on as usual. Before we realized it, the 4th of July was here, and we were heading for the parade and fireworks. I often wonder why we are always looking forward to the next event or weekend getaway.

It seems as though it's our way to get through the workweek – having something to look forward to on the weekend.

After the Independence Day celebration, I was mentally already at our next event without physically being there. We were going to Minneapolis, MN to attend the 100th Convention of the Apostolic Lutheran Church of America. It would be a time of fellowship and worship services, a time to get together with family and friends from across the country, and enjoy each other's presence around the Word of God. That weekend came and went, without a chance to slow down life. I would like to share with you one thing about that weekend regarding Cole. It was a time when Cole wanted to put to use the learning experience of watching Dad shave. He managed to get my razor and thought he needed to clean up his face. In doing so, he got a nice razor cut across his lip. What a setback when you're in a hurry to get to a church service, but we made it on time without too much trouble!

It's interesting when you look back at different experiences, and there are always those few that stick out above the rest. One of those experiences was when we were in the lunch line at the convention. When you're standing in a long line, you don't have a whole lot to do beside visit and communicate with those around you. My aunt said something to me when I was standing in the line holding Cole in my arms. It was one of those things that at the time, and unless God gave you a reason to, would never enter your mind. She mentioned to me what a blessing it is to have healthy children. I immediately agreed, as if I could possibly know what it was like to have anything other than a healthy child.

Wow! What a statement that was. At the time I didn't know what it was like to have an unhealthy child. So often I would hear of so and so being sick or someone having this or that health problem. How my heart and soul would just skip right by the thought of them. Maybe I would commit to saying I would send some prayers on their behalf, only to forget by the time I would rest my weary head on the pillow and spill out *my* wish list to God. I was so shallow in my mind, thinking that everything was going according to *my* plan. And it was, according to the calendar and schedule of events in my life.

As the calendar had it, we were soon off to our family reunion in South Carolina the next weekend. We packed our luggage strategically to fit into the small Cherokee 180 plane that was our transportation. Like most general aviation pilots, I often would find any excuse to enjoy the freedom of flight. This trip was no exception. With Cole's and my personal passion for flying, we had to make the journey as a family! We departed from IWD (India Whiskey Delta) early Thursday morning, packed in like sardines with two car seats in the back for Cole and our young daughter, Chaneille. Luckily for us the weather was nice, and the kids were tired and slept for most of the first leg of the trip. We landed to take a break at an air museum in central Illinois that has old, retired airplanes from different decades of warfare. I can't forget walking on the tarmac with our two munchkins in front, holding each other's hand and seeing the huge war birds covering the horizon.

Air museum in Illinois one week before Cole's diagnosis

Before long, we were back in the air on the way to our next stop in Tennessee, prior to our final destination in McCormick, SC.

We had an absolutely wonderful weekend enjoying the weather and each other at the reunion. It was a little hotter than what I was used to, coming from the Upper Peninsula of Michigan, but nonetheless it was nice and the golf course was well kept. Like most times when our family gets together, we arranged to make it to the golf course. It's not like my golf game reflects any time actually spent golfing, because I will admit I am far from being a Tiger Woods. However, the reason I have to explain this golf trip is because I managed to hurt my back swinging too hard on one of my drives off the tee box. The story of my injured back was told at Cole's funeral three months later.

Once again the weekend went by like the wind and we were on our way home. I never thought about the fact that we were going to be in South Carolina in the middle of summer with absolutely no air conditioning in the plane. When we climbed aboard the plane, the temperature was 110 degrees, and the sweat was pouring off of my face within minutes. Once we were airborne, the heat wasn't too bad. It wasn't long before we had to stop for the night, partly because my back hurt so much. I could hardly stand a few more minutes on the plane, let alone hours. We eventually made it back to the local Gogebic-Iron County airport without any problems. I was back at work the next morning and as usual looked forward to our next weekend adventure. This time we had a camping trip planned with my cousin and his family. However, God had a different plan for us that was far greater than my schedule.

From Caring Bridge Readers

Cole was such an inspiration and allowed me to care for him so deeply even though I have never known him. Cole's story touched my heart in ways

I never thought was possible. It took three-year-old Cole's journey to show me that God can unite thousands of people in prayer throughout the world to "BE THERE" for a little boy and his family in time of need, through endless hours, days, and weeks of prayer.

He made me realize that life can change in an instant and we are not in control of our lives at all. He taught me to love a little harder, hug a little longer, and smile a little brighter. I accept each new day as a blessing because this world is just a temporary place for you and me. Cole's legacy will live on in my heart forever.

– From Indiana

When I was first introduced to Cole, I learned of a sweet, three-year-old boy who loved to fish, cherished his Mommy and Daddy, loved airplanes, had a heart filled with laughter, and adored his little sister. As time went on, I learned that this same three-year-old boy was blessed with an abundance of precious gifts from God. Cole was a boy who demonstrated compassion, kindness, patience, empathy, love, and above all, a faith in God. Cole provided me the clarity to see that I need to use his teachings and start nurturing my relationships for they are the Here and Now. Thank you, Cole.

– From Wisconsin

Chapter 2

Cole's Early Diagnosis

July 24, 2008, was a very typical day at work pouring sidewalks in the city of Ashland, WI. Everything seemed to be what I used to call a good day. To me, a good day was nice weather, lots of production at work, being ahead of schedule, and my wife and kids waiting for me at home. It didn't take long for me to realize how shallow my idea of a "good day" would soon become.

I got home from work that evening a little earlier than usual. When I pulled into the driveway, all I remember now is Cole and my daughter, Chaneille, running to the big front window of our home to welcome me. After the greeting at the window, Cole would run to the entryway where he would open the door for Dad. That day was no different. With the help of Mom, he quickly opened the door for me and proceeded with his typical bear hug. My wife was a little surprised that I was home early. I wanted to give her a break, so I suggested that we should order pizza and eat it on the dock at Sunday Lake. Without much hesitation, she agreed. We soon had Cole's fishing pole in the car and we were on our way.

The pizza was excellent as always, and the weather couldn't have been better. It was one of those days where you can really sit down and enjoy God's wonderful creation. Cole's excitement was enough to radiate through our souls. His smile was from ear to ear, and his little trot out to the dock was simply priceless to behold. Everything was going right, and Cole had his fishing hook in the water. It was the first time that I realized he had more patience than I did. The boy was three years old and already a much better fisherman than I think I could ever be.

That evening was the first time he caught a fish. I remember sitting next to him when his bobber sank, and I couldn't help but laugh at his chuckle. Soon he was reeling in his whale. It was actually a little crappie, about four inches long, but the fish would grow every time Cole mentioned how big it was. By the end of the night, he had two fish to his credit. It was awesome to be able to be with him and see how excited he was to catch two fish. On the way home, all we heard about was his fish and how his cousin, Aubrey, only caught one fish a few days before. He was a proud fisherman.

Cole holding his whale. A grin I will never forget!

It was a night that may have just slipped by if we hadn't taken advantage of it. Little did we know it was the last time we would ever be able to enjoy this type of fun with our son. It was growing close to 9:30 p.m. when Cole mentioned that he had to go to the bathroom. As he was sitting on the toilet, he began to complain of "owies" in his abdomen and that he just couldn't go. His complaints began to grow into small whimpers and eventually into cries. You couldn't help but notice his scowling face. We proceeded to get him ready for bed as usual, and without much complaining, he cooperated.

During the night, Cole got up several times to use the bathroom, nothing out of the ordinary. Shortly after this, Moireen began feeling sick with flu-like symptoms. Both of us assumed that Cole was coming down with a bug and had passed it on. That night and the next day went on as usual. Since Moireen and Cole were both sick, they spent the day resting in bed, with Cole going in and out of his bad moments. We noticed his abdomen was very tense and maybe enlarged enough to cause concern. The thought of taking him to the doctor seemed to be like an overkill in this situation. You know how it is when you can't decide whether or not you can justify the cost of an emergency room visit because of suspecting the flu or a cold.

It wasn't until my wife was on the phone with her mother that she mentioned taking Cole to see the doctor. Her mother wondered if his enlarged abdomen could have resulted from his appendix bursting or some other bizarre thing. I recall sitting on the couch with Cole at about 11:00 that night when he mentioned going to see the doctor. Cole's exact words were, "I wanna go see the doctor." I guess the ER (emergency room) was calling our name.

When we walked into the ER, I was holding Cole on my shoulder much like any father would hold a tired three-year-old. The thought of going to the hospital was a little against my better judgment. Because our community is served by a smaller hospital, I recognized many familiar faces on the staff when we arrived. Not knowing what the problem was, they asked me, and I remember feeling very awkward telling them my boy has a stomachache. I thought they would look at him, perhaps prescribe some antibiotics, and away we would go. Part of me was saying that since it was already creeping toward 3:00 a.m. and we were still there, something must not be right.

They ran Cole through a series of x-rays and MRI's (magnetic resonance imaging), during which his pain continued to worsen. It wasn't long before he had his first IV (intravenous) and was receiving morphine. The morphine would relax him for the short term, sufficient to get him resting and to fall asleep. Cole laid there with me until both of us fell asleep on the hospital bed.

It was 5:30 a.m. when the doctor woke me up by shaking my hand that was around Cole's head. Fortunately, Cole managed to stay sleeping through the next few minutes. The doctor said, "Aaron, I'm afraid I have some bad news for you! I sent Cole's test results to a specialist in Minneapolis for study. Even though they are preliminary results, Cole has a tumor in his abdomen." I remember lying there in complete shock, thinking that my family had never experienced any related health problems.

I was waiting to wake up from my bad dream, but unfortunately the dream would only continue to get worse. I turned my head to look at this absolutely innocent child and just began to weep. All I could hear from the doctor was that he was so sorry. I can assure you that when I came in 6 1/2 hours earlier, a tumor was nothing I could have even begun to imagine. The dreaded phone call was being awaited by my wife, who was at home with Chaneille. That's when it all began – the world suddenly stopping with the phone calls to the immediate family. Six o'clock on Saturday morning was not your typical time for phone calls to Mom and Dad and aunts and uncles.

It wasn't long before the hospital was making arrangements for our transportation to a different facility. The ambulance was on its way, and before much could be said, my wife and I were on our way with Cole to a hospital in Marshfield, WI. The feeling of shock that I experienced at that time was more than I can ever explain. Cole was just such an awesome kid to have to be going through this. So often people would tell us what a good job we had done with Cole. Let me tell you it's easy, when you're dealing with an angel and God's blessings. From the day Cole was born, I sensed there was something different about him. What was it? At that time we had no idea.

The three-hour ride in the ambulance was oddly different. Considering that I had been up throughout the night, with the exception of a few hours in the morning, it was a ride with many mixed feelings. There were feelings of frustration and the questions of, "Why me? Why now? Why Cole?" along with many other questions that raced through my mind. Battling physical tiredness as well as mental exhaustion was enough to make my head spin. I still think the ride was the longest three hours that I can remember. It was also a time when I put my brain into a learning mode by listening to what the paramedics had to say.

Walking into the oncology department of the hospital was an experience of which I was gladly unaware. It was like it was our own little section in the pediatrics area of the hospital and almost made us feel special. Then it dawned on me that being in that section has absolutely nothing special written on it. It was more like it was a little less fortunate, or not as lucky of a section. It was not long until reality hit me that this was something serious and we weren't going to get a "get cured quick pill" and go home.

It was Saturday, which in my opinion now, is not a good time to be at a hospital when you may have to stay over the weekend or longer. For the next two days, absolutely no progress was made in determining a diagnosis for Cole's tumor. We had to wait until Monday, wondering what this thing was while he just had his blood pressure and tempera-ture checked. I'm sure many other parents who have been in this situation can relate to the frustrations you can feel on a weekend stay at the hospital.

At the time, nobody had any idea that Cole had adrenocortical carcinoma; it was expected to be neuroblastoma. Unfortunately, those few days of waiting, along with the next two weeks, would prove to have a significant effect on the tumor's progress and its growth.

From A CaringBridge Reader

I work with a guy that one day came up to me and asked me to pray for Cole. He explained to me how to get to Cole's site on CaringBridge. I had never heard about it before. I immediately was brought down to my knees as I was deeply touched by Cole. I became a prayer warrior. I never knew I could pray the way I found myself doing. No one in my life had ever touched me this way. I had some dear family members taken from me and have experienced some very rough times, and never did I find myself like this.

It is so hard to try to explain. I now find myself talking with God steadily. My faith deepened. I had no idea it could. God changed my life through Cole. I found myself compelled to talk with others about this. I didn't understand and thought it was just me. I would get an update from you and read a few of the other people's entries and was shocked to find out it wasn't just me. There are thousands of us! It shocked me. I was and am amazed. I would read some of the entries and get the shivers, and tears would fill my eyes as I was reading words I could have written. It was describing how I was feeling to a T, how I had changed and was changing.

*This young man, **COLE,** has changed us. I find it absolutely amazing. What an awesome God. **How miraculous!!!** It sort of freaks me out as I think* *of you and your family so often. Many mornings I awake and pray for each of you before I even put my feet on the floor.*

Every single day I find myself thinking about you and praying many times a day. I simply am a better person now. I love more. I thought I loved all I could, but I love more and deeper. I am so thankful for all I have.

I have two grandsons who will never look the same. I now see Cole in them. I pray that God will speak to them the way He is now speaking to me. It is so awesome to feel so loved like this. I honestly thought I was a good person and Christian. I had no idea God could love me more. He does. I can't believe how when I now read and study God's Word, I find myself highlighting something and writing Cole's name by it. I have tears in my eyes as I try to find the words to describe myself now. I love Cole so much and cannot wait to meet him. I thank God so very much for Cole!!

– From Minnesota

Chapter 3

Start of a Roller Coaster Ride

Sunday, July 27, 2008, 2:38 p.m.

Monday will bring a very important and busy day for Cole. The tumor turned out to be malignant. Many of the tests that will be given to see the severity of his cancer start tomorrow, so PLEASE continue to pray for him. Some of the tests are: (1) Bone marrow aspiration and biopsy; (2) CT (computed tomography) scan; (3) Bone scan; (4) Echocardiogram (a baseline measurement of his heart to determine its condition); (5) Blood tests, for checking the HGB (hemoglobin) level in his blood – his high counts are a little low, so they are continuing to monitor this.

Throughout these tests, he will be sedated. In his current state, he is still receiving pain meds. He appears to be in good spirits, possibly better than his mother and I are feeling at this time. He told us that he has no "owies," but for those of you who know him, even if he did, he would say that he doesn't have any. I was lying next to him this morning with tears in my eyes, and he wiped them with his fist and said, "DADDY, I DON'T HAVE OWIES

ANYMORE." May God continue to comfort him! Bye, Love you ALL.

Aaron

It was the uncertainty of not knowing that so often made us feel frustrated and anxious – anxious to receive any news or results from any and all of the tests Cole had been given. I realized the gift that God had given us when on the morning that I was lying next to him, he leaned over and wiped my tears. To see the love of a child, in pure humbleness, lay his burdens aside to reach out to me and care for my tears, was humbling.

So often when we would be sitting in church and hear a touching message that would bring me to tears, it would be Cole that would wipe away my tears, put his hands on my cheeks, look me straight in the eyes, and smile. He was much more than a *SON* to us. He was our strength and encourager – my guardian angel. When Cole was born, it was the first time that I can truly say that God took my heart and transformed me from the inside out. For those of us that have had the joy of having a child, it is something that is second to none.

My mind cannot help but think of the thousands of people who like to think that there is nothing wrong with abortion. You know that we live in hard times when trees or animals somehow get to have more rights than a precious child – an innocent child that is unable to speak out on his or her behalf against those who take their lives. If there is anybody who is considering an abortion, please reconsider. I know we can help find a loving home for that innocent life. After all, you don't know but that child could be your "angel" here on earth.

As I am writing this page of the book, the *Caring-Bridge* website, which I have not yet mentioned, is going wild with people trying to think of a legacy for Cole's life.

Over 150 guestbook entries on different ideas and suggestions that are well thought out and prayed about have been submitted. It must be a "God thing" that this book is being written because I had started writing several days before I had posted anything on suggestions for Cole's legacy.

It was rather ironic that so many have come up with the idea of writing a book. God's ways are far greater than our ways. Many people had suggested a title *of "To the Moon and Back, My Son's Journey With Adrenocortical Carcinoma."* The eventual title of this book evolved from many suggestions.

The *CaringBridge* website is and has been a place of comfort and strength, a place to vent our feelings, and to cry. The website has been so wonderful throughout our journey that I cannot say enough good things about it. My cousin, Julie, had called me after she heard the news about Cole and mentioned this "caring bridge" and how we could create an actual website for Cole. Quite frankly, I didn't really think too much about it other than giving her the blessing of proceeding with the website.

I remember our conversation when she had finished creating it. She had the story of Cole on the welcome page, and it was really neat to see. I had no idea that it would soon be another source of venting throughout this whole experience. I actually remember thinking that it was sort of ridiculous, because how in the world would people ever get the name of the site?

Little did I know that God had a much greater plan with the site than I could have ever imagined – a plan that would produce over half a million hits in eight weeks. That is more than 8,461.5 hits per day, 352 hits per hour, 24 hours a day, for almost nine weeks. It would eventually add up to almost eight hits on Cole's website every minute of every day that he was in the hospital.

The news traveled like wildfire, piercing the hearts of those who heard about Cole. It was only the hand of God that could have come close to making something so real to people across the country. But God didn't stop in our country with most of the 50 states accounted for on this site. He also touched base with many other countries and continents.

My mind kept going back to the time when there were as little as 500 hits on the website. Even at that time, I couldn't fathom how so many people could be in touch with Cole. For some reason, God blessed Cole's story so much that it seemed like every person who read his journal was immediately a part of the family from the first time they laid eyes on Cole. I have nothing else to say about the site other than the fact that there is no doubt in my mind, or anyone else's, that this could not have been caused by anything other than the blessed hand of God.

Monday, July 28, 2008, 3:42 p.m.

We just talked with the doctor about some of the test results. It breaks me apart to have to say this, but the news is much worse than we had hoped. The tumor is now 6" x 4", with confirmation that it is spreading into his liver. It also has been found in his lungs, with pieces being more than one inch, and in his IVC (inferior vena cava), which is a main artery leading to his heart. So far, all the news has been bad news.

Aaron

It has never ceased to amaze me how it seemed like every time we would get reports back from the doctors, everything was like a giant snowball, rolling downhill, continuing to pick up speed and size, as it made its way to the bottom. It had only been two days since we heard that the tumor was approaching the size of an adult's fist; now it was suddenly 6" x 4". Talk about shock and awe! His stomachache was turning into an all out attack on the liver, lungs, IVC, and abdomen just four days after fishing at Sunday Lake where we watched Cole catch his first fish.

It was not easy to accept, considering that at this time he was still very much in tune with reality, acting much like himself. The few videos that were played at his funeral and displayed on his website with him talking on the phone discussing life with his cousins, were taken during this time. He always would ask everyone how they were doing and very humbly tell them that he was sick and in the hospital. At one point he even called it his home.

Everything was getting to be routine for him, as far as the nurses and their schedules were concerned. Considering he had only been there three days, I thought he was doing pretty well. When the nurses would come in to take his blood pressure, he was already raising his arm so they could wrap the cuff around it.

It felt like we were back in school again when we received pages and pages of different literature regarding the oncology department and neuroblastoma. At this point we still had no idea what the exact diagnosis was, but the signs and preliminary evidence showed that we were up against the disease called neuroblastoma. This is what the most common cancer found in children was called. We spent much time researching and reading about this cancer.

One of the things that we did more than read was to worry. I guess as parents we have a right to be concerned, but as Christians, the Word reminds us not to worry. Moireen would always remind me not to worry, for God will take care of tomorrow. Take the sparrows of the air, for example. God simply takes care of them.

I found myself constantly getting caught up with thoughts that now seem so insignificant. I distinctly remember the doctors telling us that they would have to place a central line in Cole, otherwise known as the "Hickman" catheter, which is used to administer medicines.

I thought of many things when they told us the news of the implanting of this central line. One of the first things was that Cole was not going to be able to swim with all of his cousins. One of his favorite pastimes during the summer was to go swimming in a lake or at Grandma's and Grandpa's pool. Now I can look back and think how I spent all that time and all of those hours getting one step closer to gray hair by worrying about something so insignificant. I guess at the time thinking that Cole would have a permanent line installed in his chest was not exactly a small thing.

Looking back at the thought of the "line," it so often reminds me of how we look at our lives. How can we go through our lives worrying about things that have so little value, when you consider the core values of life? It's unfortunate that it took something so significant in my life to make me stop running, trying to get ahead of the paycheck to paycheck routine, living just to gain something that I now realize has so little value.

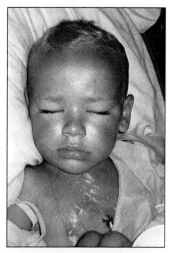

Many nights I would worry about work and how this or that was going to be able to get done the next day. It was those nights when I wasn't there for Cole, to "run the corners" with him or to simply spend quality time with my family. The Hickman line would soon be put in, and it wasn't long before we could see the blessings of it in a natural sense for Cole.

Cole after installation of Hickman catheter

Wednesday, July 30, 2008, 10:24 a.m.

Hello to all of you from Aaron and Moireen. We are anxiously waiting to hear how the surgery is going. We left Cole this morning as he fell asleep in his bed with Mom and me and the Hot Wheels that he received as a present. Cole is very appreciative of all the gifts he has been getting. Yesterday we got back from his ultrasound test and entered his room to see it filled with balloons. Cole's smile was one we could all melt over.

We have been waiting for several hours to hear from the doctor. In the meantime, we logged onto the site to update his journal and were bombarded with notes, songs, and scripture, all of which are so encouraging to us.

Hours later, when we finally got to the journal, we were interrupted by the doctor who told us that the surgery went well and we would be able to see Cole in several minutes. The amazing thing to us is that one little man, who's a part of a bigger person named God, can bring thousands of people together that are miles apart.

It's interesting to me how we as humans think that we can handle every situation and do not realize that God may have a different plan. For us, it was Cole's illness, and for many others who have been in a situation similar to ours, we are completely helpless as parents.

Thousands of visitors checked this site and wished they could do something to help. We are immediately humbled by this and realize that all we can do is pray and look up to the Author and Creator of us all.

Aaron

From CaringBridge Readers

Before I came across Cole's prayer request, I was beginning to sound like a broken record when I would pray at night. It seemed like lately I was asking for patience from God too often in the way I would deal with situations in my life. Cole taught me that we don't know what the days will bring and we need to treat each day as if it were our last... no one is guaranteed a tomorrow. I think before I speak and don't fret over the little things. Thanks to Cole, I have more patience, speak kinder words, and have realized that God does have a plan for each of us, and there is no need to worry about anything. His legacy has touched our whole family: Love a Little Harder, Hug a Little Longer, Smile a Little Brighter and thank God for everything I have... and also "BE THERE."

– From Wisconsin

If I had to sum up how Cole has changed me, it would be to say that I now see life as minutes, days, and hours, instead of weeks and years. Our life is in limbo right now as my husband gets his Master's Degree and I study for the CPA exam. He is pastor of a church in Tennessee and we are considering moving, etc. I have often thought that I would be so glad when everything settles down in a "couple of years." Cole has made me realize that the future is important to consider, but what we have is now. Even Grayson doesn't leave us due to tragedy. He will never be two again and these precious moments that I have now with him will not return. Through your example, I have slowed everything down from thinking about life in a "couple of years" to living in the present and trying to BE THERE every minute that I have with my child, not just be there physically, but mentally, emotionally, and spiritually. Thank you for sharing your precious gift with us.

— From North Carolina

At the very moment that I looked into those beautiful blue eyes, I knew that I was looking at someone special. I would have never thought that a three-year-old little boy that I had never even met would soon be changing my life in such an important way. Cole instantly consumed my thoughts, my prayers and my heart. Reading his story day after day taught me lessons that I didn't even know that I needed. He taught me to love my children more when I didn't even think that it was possible to love them more than I already did. He taught me to cherish every smile, every laugh, every hug, and every moment with my children and loved ones.

He taught me to accomplish what our Lord has in store for us, no matter what the circumstances may be. He taught me to really LOVE a stranger. He taught me to teach my children how to love and pray for someone that they had never met. He taught me how to spread the Word of God by sharing his story with others. That sweet little boy has touched me so deeply that words will never truly express my feelings about him. Thank you, thank you, and thank you for sharing your most precious possession with the world.

— From Texas

Chapter 4

The Church as One, in Prayer

If you ever had to bring your child to the hospital for any sort of substantial surgery, you will be able to relate to exactly how I felt prior to Cole's biopsy. It was a feeling that brings you down to a place where you realize that there is absolutely nothing you can do for them. I remember watching him get wheeled out of the room and getting an overwhelming feeling of helplessness. You can probably relate to times when your child has fallen and bumps their head or any other part of their body; the times when all you need to do is kiss the damaged limb or spot and everything is miraculously better. It was that sort of feeling I kept getting from Cole when he would look at us. It was almost like he just wanted a kiss and all of a sudden everything would be magically okay. It was the most humbling experience that I can ever recall. This was the first major surgery that we had experienced. We had no idea of the upcoming surgeries and touching experiences that were still to come each time Cole would get wheeled away to the operating room.

This was the first time that we had to wait for Cole in the waiting room for over three hours. Fortunately, we had something to keep us busy during this time. Once again *CaringBridge* came to the rescue. Our original thought was to post an update during our wait. When we went to the guestbook we were overwhelmed by encouraging letters and scripture. It was wonderful, as you can tell from the previous journal entry we began at the beginning of our wait. We stayed glued to the guestbook until the doctors came to visit us. At times like these, the *CaringBridge* family was truly our strength and support.

I remember hearing families tell their stories about an experience in the hospital or a tough time that they had gone through. They would so often get strength through the prayers of others as they could feel the body of Christ working. I will be the first to admit that the body of Christ is your strength in times of trouble. The Word of God doesn't lie when it tells us in Ecclesiastes 4:10: *"For if they fall, the one will lift up his fellow: but woe to him that is alone when he falleth; for he hath not another to help him up."* I experienced that love from the body of Christ firsthand, and this is most certainly why God created the Church.

The Church is so much more than just a building where we gather on Sunday to hear the message. It is and should be alive and living daily as a body of believers, lending a hand to those in need, picking up the fallen, and encouraging them along the way. It feels so close after this experience that it makes my heart cry for those folks who have to go through difficulties in life, particularly something like this, without being a part of the body of Christ. I can't help but believe that through our experience, God was most certainly glorified. It was through the life of one little, innocent child, who just happens to be my son, that God brought our whole community and many people in the nation together.

I remember lying on the uncomfortable hospital bed/bench in Cole's room just thanking God for my being a part of such a family. I think of how I was as a person when I would see somebody that I hardly knew, and I would begin to judge them without comprehending that I was actually doing it. It's not that I would intentionally place people in different categories. It just happens, and I'm sure you can relate to this. So many times someone that I knew from our town would sign our guestbook, and some of the things they would write amazed me. It was such an evident reminder to me of how dangerous it is to have this preconceived perception of someone whom you do not really even know.

Speaking of not even knowing, it causes me to think about the people that we assume we know well. For example, our own immediate families, or our congregational members, or maybe even just close friends. How well do we actually know them? We might know of them, who they are by name, what they do by occupation, or whether we think of them as having any sort of stature in this life. We are very prone to have these shallow thoughts of and relationships with one another.

I have begun to realize personally how little our "stature thermometer" means in the whole scope of life. What about really getting to know people as God wants us to know them? How about becoming their accountability partners? Do we even know them by their hearts, or just by their names? I am ashamed to say that I know most people only by their names. It is no wonder that so many struggle with so many different things when it seems as if no one is interested in the "nuts and bolts" of their life.

In my life, I would continue to go to church every Sunday and participate in the Youth Group, but meanwhile have a completely fake wall on the outside. That's what I mean when I ask, "Do we really know each other?" No one would really have gotten to know me. I may have been known, but what really mattered was slipping by the wayside. As Christians, we know that these questions are difficult, and we know they can convict us. Like so much of everything in this world, we want to take the easy way out. It's no wonder why so much in this life is all about making it easier and gaining more material goods. I feel that we are just getting accustomed to taking the easy way out, including our personal walk with the Lord.

How can that be possible? Why would we want to hear these words spoken to us on that last day: *"Depart from me, ye cursed, into everlasting fire prepared for the devil and his angels." (Matthew 25:41),* instead of the words: *"Come, ye blessed of my Father, inherit the kingdom prepared for you from the foundation of the world." (Matthew 25:34)*

We all have a choice to make whether or not we want to live a life according to God's Word. Perhaps we need to change the way we think about this life by eliminating the rat race and stop chasing the almighty dollar that has no value to anything important in life. When one comes to a place in life where the end is in sight, one realizes firsthand what's important. You have to understand that I am not saying that we need not take care of ourselves, expecting everything to be free, and therefore we don't have to work in this life. What I'm saying is that we need to have our priorities in line.

I want to share the words with you from one of the nurses at the hospital in Marshfield, WI. She explained to me that she has been a nurse for almost forty years and has yet to meet an atheist on their deathbed. Yes, it might say atheist on their medical records, but as she told me, she has yet to see one person who at the end does not look up to the God, Who is the Author and Maker of all things. When you have no place to turn and no strength of your own, you have nothing else that you can do but look UP!

This reminds me of the first time I did a solo flight in my training to get my pilot's license. When I got into the cockpit, taxied to the end of the runway, and took off, it didn't take long for me to know on whom I had to rely. There was no one else around, just my instructor, who was watching from 1,000 feet below. In moments like this, you immediately come to terms with God and realize that He is the only one Who is always with you, REGARDLESS.

Wednesday, July 30, 2008, 1:40 p.m. (PDT)

Wow! Reading through everyone's comments I find myself wiping my eyes so much that I can barely read them. It is amazing when the church comes together and works like God intended it to do. I was text messaging Aaron this morning, and as you all know, the surgery went well. Thank you Jesus! They successfully implanted the Hickman line and Cole was recovering well. One thing that touched my heart is that when Cole woke up, his first words were, "Mom and Dad, I want you to lay with me." So Aaron and Moireen crawled into the bed and Cole whispered to Aaron, "Dad, I want you to have a blanket so you're not cold." It touched Aaron so much that Cole was worried more about him than himself. Oh what a precious little boy!

Now the waiting game starts again. It can be up to 36 hours before they will know the results of the biopsy. Please pray for them as they sit and wait. Someone posted this verse in the guestbook, and I think it is so fitting right now that I'm going to make it the verse of the day: Isaiah 41:10: "Don't be afraid, for I am with you. Don't be discouraged, for I am your God. I will strengthen you and help you. I will hold you up with my victorious right hand." Praise Jesus!

Cousin Julie

We were extremely surprised to see our doctor come in to visit us early Thursday afternoon. He had received the results of Cole's biopsy 24 hours sooner than expected.

Unfortunately, things were not changing for that snowball that was on its way down the hill. Again, it just seemed like all of the odds were against us. This next post was one that I could not even write because I didn't have the strength to accept the facts that the doctor had been giving us. After Cole was recovering from the biopsy, we thought that things were going well. The comments that Cole continued to make assured us that he was still the same boy we knew before the surgery. His tenderness and spirit had not even begun to get shattered at this point. He was still the same Cole.

Thursday, July 31, 2008, 1:55 p.m. (PDT)

My heart is heavy right now, as I have just gotten off the phone with Aaron. They just received the results from the biopsy. It is worse than they were hoping for. Little Cole has adrenocortical carcinoma. It is a cancer that is typically found in adults. Aaron understood that it is so rare that one in a million cancer patients are diagnosed with it, and here little Cole has it. The doctors say it's even harder to treat than the neuroblastoma that they originally thought it might be. What does one even say at this point? There are no words to comfort someone whose child is diagnosed with such a thing.

A verse from Jeremiah comes to mind... it gives me so much hope and it's one of my favorite verses to think of during a time like this. Jeremiah 29:11-13... "For I know the plans I have for you," says the Lord, "they are plans for good and not disaster, to give you a future and a hope. In those days when you pray I will listen. If you look for me wholeheartedly, you will find me."

That is what we are holding onto for Cole and the family. Now is the time the battle will start. Now is when Cole needs us the most to be covering him in prayer. Now is when Aaron and Moireen will need all the help, encourage-ment, hope and prayers that can possibly be given. Now the real battle starts. There is now a name to this awful cancer that has plagued Cole's body. Now we can pray directly for God to heal his body.

Aaron said that Cole hasn't been feeling too well since his surgery. He mostly sleeps and is in a lot of pain. They have increased his pain medication three times from what it was previously. They will also be starting the chemo-therapy tonight. So I ask of everyone, please keep sending them messages and keep praying! Pray, pray, pray! That is the best thing we can do for them right now.

Cousin Julie

When the doctor first started talking, he mentioned that he had the results of the biopsy. He said. "We have some good news and bad news. Which would you like first?" We said the good news, and he began telling us that the cancer was found to not be neuroblastoma. Wow, what a blessing we thought after reading pages and pages of the effects and odds of winning the fight against such a disease. Then he dropped the "bomb." He told us that the bad news was that Cole had adrenocortical carcinoma (ACC). Okay, whatever that is, I thought. Little did I know the odds of winning the battle against ACC were slim to none. For the first time I remember having the feeling that we were going to lose him to cancer, of all things. The thought of having to bury my child slowly began sinking in.

It wasn't long before the word spread, and we suddenly had thousands of prayer warriors on our behalf. The doctor assured us that they were going to do everything that they could to fight this for Cole. He explained to us that they wanted to start the chemotherapy later that evening to get things rolling. The plan was that Cole would have five days on chemotherapy, then up to two weeks off, depending on his blood count and other stats. Immediately all of the stories began coming into my mind about the side effects of chemo. I couldn't help but think about the side effects that we were reading about in the handouts the hospital gave us. Trying to picture Cole losing his hair was something that wasn't really setting too well, even though it was so insignificant in the whole scheme of things.

All of the odds were against us on this disease. There was only a 0.2% chance that he could have even gotten ACC. Genetically, there is a 6 to 1 ratio between girls and boys getting the disease. That brought the statistics much further from reality and meant that his odds were less than a 0.02% chance of even getting ACC. The only direction that any of the doctors had for us at this time is to start the chemotherapy. The thought of surgery on the tumor had sort of been ruled out at this point because the tumor had wrapped itself around Cole's aorta. They felt that surgery would be much too risky to perform and recommended that chemotherapy be tried first to see what it could do. The start of chemotherapy treatment started a whole new world for us.

From A CaringBridge Reader

It's obvious how much Cole has touched so many lives. Something has come over me over the last couple of months. I am a mother of three..., 7, 6, & 3. When things get crazy in my house, now I deal with the chaos in a much more calm way. In the past I used to raise my voice and feel like no one (children, that is) hears me!!! My home is on a much more calm level now, even when things are CRAZY. I have to thank Cole for this.

I do hug a little tighter and do wedding kisses more often. These kisses are my kid's favorites – we look up at the sky and kiss on each other's neck. My husband and I have a beautiful wedding picture of us doing that. It has become an everyday thing now.

Thank you to your family. I still cry and pray for your family "Every Day."

– From Virginia

Chapter 5

Pray Without Ceasing

Friday, August 1, 2008 12:12 a.m.

Moireen and I sat down to quickly read the latest entries on the CaringBridge site since we haven't had a chance to read them since last night. To our amazement, we had what seemed like hundreds to read. It was a good thing that Cole happened to be sleeping; otherwise we wouldn't have made it in one sitting. Unfortunately, we haven't been able to see the smiles of Cole for the last two days. Like the Word says, when one stumbles there is another to lift us up. And that is exactly what all of you have been to us. So many times I feel like sobbing, but I find myself unable to do so because my bulk supply of tears has been depleted. Then I realize that Cole needs us to be strong.

Moireen had a thought that I want to share with all of you, being that many of you are mothers and can relate to this. We were transporting Cole back to his room from surgery. After seeing him go through everything in the last few days, she said to me... "After all of this, how must it have been for Jesus' mother, Mary, to stand back and watch her Son get beaten, torn, spit upon, mocked, and tortured the way He was... and not being able to do anything, knowing that this was the will of God..." May we have comfort in knowing that this is indeed the will of God for Cole for reasons that we do not know right now. Thank you for continuing to sign our guestbook!!!

Aaron

Friday morning was the start of the most severe pain that we had to witness in Cole. There really are and will be no real words to be able to describe the feelings that we had when all we could do was to hold Cole and give him words from our feeble mouths that it was going to be okay. Everything that we had heard about the horrors of chemotherapy were slowly coming true. To this day, we still are not sure if it was the result of the chemo or if it was the tumor in his abdomen bothering him. He would just scream in pain, moaning and groaning that his stomach hurt. To hear him tell you he has "owies" was not something that I could handle very easily. He would look me directly in the eyes as we were holding him and murmur the words, "Help me, Daddy!!" The pain was so strong that it brings me to tears to even write about it now.

"Why in the world should a child have to go through this? WHY? Why Cole?" The boy who was someone I could only dream about. "Why us, Lord?" It was a time when I just prayed to God to please take him home – please spare him from this pain and torture. Looking back at those days it was clearly evident that God was not through with him and his ministry. At that time there were around 30,000 hits on his *CaringBridge* site. If God would have answered my prayers at that time, it would have left over half a million people out of the loop of Cole's story. It was also a time that, looking back, we realized that God's plans are the best, regardless of what we might think.

Friday, August 1, 2008, 3:30 p.m. (PDT)

Dear friends... Please pray without ceasing this day and hour for Cole. He has been in so much pain last night and today. I have to dig as deep as I can to find the courage and strength to even write this, but I know that if God can hear prayers from the thousands, He has the ability to move mountains. In all, I'm begging and pleading that he doesn't have to scream and say "owie" constantly! It seems that no matter how much pain medicine they give him, it doesn't seem to be working. I will not update any more pictures so we all can remember Cole the way he used to be. May God hear our prayers.

"OH DEAR GOD, I CRY OUT TO YOU THAT YOU MAY COMFORT AND STRENGTHEN HIM. HE IS IN SO MUCH PAIN AS YOU ALREADY KNOW. PLEASE HELP HIM, LORD. IF IT IS YOUR WILL TO TAKE HIM, PLEASE DO SO BEFORE WE HAVE TO WATCH THIS ANYMORE. I COMMIT HIM TO YOU NOW AT THIS TIME. AS I AM THE FATHER TO COLE, AND YOU ARE A FATHER TO US ALL, PLEASE HEAR MY PRAYER. MAY WE ALL PRAY A PRAYER FOR COLE NOW, WHEREVER WE ARE." Waiting at heaven's gate...

Aaron

53

The above is the last update that Aaron tried posting this morning, but it didn't work, so I am posting it now. It breaks my heart so much to hear a father's agony over his son. It makes me realize how much God was in agony over His Son, Jesus. I am begging you all to pray for Cole! That's all we can do at this point! As tears flow and fears increase, I am reminded that God promises to be with them and He is faithful! I believe God's promises are true. Please keep sending the messages and scriptures and comments. It not only is uplifting to them but to thousands of others. Please pray!

Cousin Julie

People from all over the country began to pray and get on board with Cole and pledged to pray for him through this time. The news spread across the world in a way that could only be by the direct hand of God. People began to drop their own personal problems and put their energy and emotion towards Cole. It was just amazing how a three-year-old boy had the ability to open people's homes and come into their families and hearts in such an angelic way. We would spend countless hours reading every entry written in the guestbook. Many entries were from people that we had no ties to whatsoever. Slowly we began to hear from people from every walk of life and many church denominations. All around the world people were getting on their knees to pray for one boy. We were getting messages from Finland, Australia, France, South Africa, Kenya, Jordan, Iraq, Sweden, Canada, Guatemala, Japan, Russia, United Kingdom, and from nearly all of the fifty states. My e-mail inbox was showing some fifty e-mails a day. I had no other understanding of why Cole was making such a sudden impact around the world, except that it had to be God's hand, directing lives to have compas-

sion on this boy. I had the hardest time understanding why
God was allowing my son, Cole, to suffer so that many could come in touch and in tune with their lives. The things he had been going through just didn't seem fair. Unfortunately, the worst was yet to come.

Praying without ceasing
- Darla, WA

Saturday, August 2, 2008, 12:32 p.m.

Dear Brothers and Sisters in faith,

The latest update of Cole unfortunately is no better than the last. Cole most certainly had his worst night EVER last night. With the chemotherapy now administered, it appears Cole has some side effects that were not really expected. He began to swell throughout his entire body, so badly that his eyes were swollen shut. His thighs, legs, neck, and stomach were swollen to the point that I thought it was the end. Cole was giving us signs all night that we wouldn't see him alive again. Maybe it was our imagination, but this is what he did... Moireen gave him a kiss and told him that she loved him. With Cole quivering and shaking, he grabbed her hand, pulled it to his lips, and began kissing it. He murmured, "I LOVE YOU TO THE MOON AND BACK." Moireen and I about fell to the floor. Then he leaned forward to give both of us hugs. What a way to remember our sweet little Cole.

He began to have severe problems with his breathing, being that the cancer was attacking his lungs so strongly. The doctors have decided it would be better to incubate him. So now he lies there in your prayers and God's healing touch protecting him. Please continue to pray for COLE.

Thanks. Aaron and Moireen.

When I reread this journal, I could not stop thinking of the night that Cole spoke the line, **"I love you to the moon and back." Famous!!** I shall never forget Cole as long as I live. As we were sitting next to him looking upon his tired, weak, and now scrawny arms, my wife told him that she loved him. He could hardly move his hands in our direction but managed to muster up the strength to reach out to Moireen and grab her hand. His arms were just shaking as he pulled her hand to his face and gave her a kiss. We were already speechless from his actions as he slowly muttered these words with his scratchy voice, **"I... love... you... to... the moon and... back."**

The world stopped; all concerns and thoughts toward whoever and whatever were immediately shut off. For a brief moment I almost thought that the only people in the entire hospital were the three of us. I had never experienced such love and compassion for somebody as I did for our son at that moment. Then to top it off, he struggled to lean forward even though he was attached to the lines monitoring his vital signs, stretched out his arms and squeezed my wife and me as tightly as I think he could, given the strength he had. He held us for what felt like an hour but was probably less than a minute. There is nothing in life that can compare to the relationship we had with Cole at that time. No amount of possessions could be worth anything close to that. It was a true meaning of the word PRICELESS. The best part about

it was that it was FREE. I guess my Dad was right when he told me that the best things in life are "free."

Sunday, August 3, 2008, 6:56 p.m.

Hello. Just ten days ago things were normal in our home. It was a Thursday when I came home from work and as usual the kids ran to our front window to welcome Dad, and then Cole ran to the front door to welcome me. Our fishing story of that Thursday was covered in a previous posting. Then two hours later Cole asked to go potty, and as he sat there he began to cry about the pain in his stomach. Our lives were transformed in a minute, but at the time we couldn't realize it. Now a week and three days later, we wait with Cole as he is on a respirator and sedated. The good news is that he is beginning to look like himself again after the swelling has gone down. Also, the fluid in his lungs has lessened in volume, so he has been able to breathe a little better. All we can do is wait and trust in God's will.

We have been able to receive peace with this horrific experience, realizing that God's will can be performed. Why else would God place this little boy on the hearts of thousands of people? Maybe it's because God assures us that when part of the body hurts we all hurt. It has been a time when we can do nothing else but look to the heavens and pray. When my Dad told me yesterday that THE BEST THINGS IN LIFE ARE FREE... not material gain..., one thing that I can't get out of my mind is all the times Cole just wanted to play with Dad and I would push his dreams away and pursue my selfish desires.

The greatest free gift we have been given is the gift of grace. God gave His Son to SUFFER AND DIE for us. Let me assure you that when God watched His Son suffer, knowing that by the touch of His finger He could stop everything, it could not have been easy. Remember, God could have called Ten Thousand Angels, but instead He chose to die for you and me.

If I could give anyone one piece of advice, it would be this: If there is something that is bothering you between you and someone else, listen to your heart and make it right between you and that person. When it is all over, you can walk free of all that is on your heart and that was bothering you. Neither you nor I know what tomorrow will bring, so take care of it before it's too late. Things can change in an instant, and there is nothing we can do.

Aaron

Monday, August 4, 2008, 11:12 a.m. (PDT)

Hello to all! I am just going to post a few updates about Cole. I just talked to Aaron and he said Cole woke up a couple of times last night from his sedation. Aaron and Moireen were sleeping at the Ronald McDonald house and received a call from the nurse that Cole was asking for them. They went to the hospital and Cole mouthed, "I love you" to his Mommy and Daddy. They gave him some more medication so he is asleep again. Aaron also said that Cole seemed to only have a little bit of pain when he woke up, so that is a praise report! He has today and tomorrow left on this round of chemo, then three weeks off before starting one week of additional chemo. This is a very long road, so please continue to pray for the chemo to do its work, but also for the Lord to do his healing work in little Cole's body.

Cousin Julie

Monday, August 4, 2008, 12:43 p.m. (PDT)

The benefit dinner for Cole will be held on August 16 at the township fire hall in Ironwood, MI. If anyone has any questions, please call Amanda. Thank you so much, Amanda, and all who are helping with the dinner.

Cousin Julie

It wasn't long before people began doing things for us that was from the bottom of their hearts and out of pure kindness. A spaghetti feed was one of the many things that had been done. About two thousand showed up to support us at this event, which we thought was very good when you consider our city only has a population of a little more than 6,000. Also, a young man decided he would like to do a bake sale for Cole. Before we knew it, there was a fundraiser for kids to get haircuts, and all proceeds were going to Cole. A toy drive was being organized, and all proceeds would be donated to the hospital.

We found out that our local community was one that had a lot more to offer than we ever would have dreamed. So often this area and community would get knocked for its faults and problems, but then it was this outpouring of love that showed me how awesome it was to be a part of this community. People from all over this county area, known as the Gogebic Range, did what they could to help and support us.

The biggest and most amazing thing to me was that it didn't just stop at our community – Cole's illness went global! For some reason, people had compassion upon this little boy. One of the thoughts that came to my mind was how people from every walk of life seemed to stop and uplift children, no matter what the circumstances. Now we all know there are a few exceptions to that, considering the child abusers that we hear about on the news. But why is it that even the hardcore prisoners have compassion upon children? So often you hear how prison is not the place where you would want to be if you have abused a child. Why is that? Is it because of the child's innocence? Or is it because in the Bible, God encourages us to be like little children and learn from them?

There is something special about children that neither you nor I can put our finger on. They are a great blessing in God's eyes. Cole was no different – his angelic smile would melt the hearts of everyone that laid eyes on him. Because of the compassion everyone had upon Cole, my thoughts were completely transformed into realizing how many great people there are across our nation – and we hear so little about all of the good things they have done. I felt open to understand how skewed our national media is. There are so many good people out there doing so many good and important things across the nation, but yet it's mostly the negative things that get portrayed in the media. I truly believe that if we put our thoughts and efforts into change, our voices can be heard. It's no different than the old saying that the "squeaky wheel gets the grease." It's unfortunate, but so often this saying holds true.

My wife and I experienced this first hand at one of the hospitals when things were not getting done according to protocol and their word. When we began taking a stand, people started to listen. One thing that cannot be forgotten is that we are also representatives of Christ, and everything we do should bring Glory to His name.

From CaringBridge Readers

My oldest daughter and her husband were having problems in their marriage, but I shared Cole's site with her and she would read your journal. It pulled them together in a way that no one else has been able to do. You and Cole showed them that they need to love more, give more, pray more, and believe more. Cole has touched everyone in my family, but he helped save a marriage.

– From South Dakota

We heard about Cole from a prayer chain that we have at work. From the moment that we read history, we felt like he was part of our family too. We shared the ups and downs with you, reading from the journal every day, praying, and waiting. We have grown stronger in faith and in love as a family; it's almost a feeling that I can't describe. Cole brought back to our attention that God has His path set for us; don't look down in sorrow... look up for faith!!!

We hug a little longer and take those few extra moments in the day to tell each other that we love each other. Cole taught me to be more involved with my kids, knowing that they could all be gone in a moment. So, thank you Cole, for reminding us that God is there for us always, to have faith, love as hard as you can, hug as hard as you can, until we all meet in heaven and spend eternity with our Creator! Much love and blessings for sharing Cole's story with us.

– From New Hampshire

Chapter 6

A Personal Testimony

Monday, August 4, 2008, 9:25 p.m.

Cole is still hanging in there, showing us how much stronger he is than I know I would be if I were in his shoes. It seems as though Cole is continuing to look more like his pictures. Every day that we get to see Cole open his eyes, it's a miracle and an answer to thousands of prayers that have stormed to the heavens. We read and dwell upon the words that so many of you have been compelled to write. But too often our eyes are fixed upon Aaron and Moireen and the strength that we have as parents. Let me tell you that the strength that we have as earthly vessels is absolutely nothing. We praise God for giving us the strength to make it through day by day. It is by His grace that we are able to stand.

People... the glory needs to be to God. Do you think that nearly 17,000 hits on his website are because of Cole? Not entirely – it is because we all have compassion, and in times like these, we can all look up to heaven to glorify God for our personal families. We wonder why God let this happen to such an innocent little boy. But this is why I believe it happened: for ME to realize my selfishness and to be taken out of the mold of being so comfortable in living my daily life.

Do you think that life can go by where everything is just right? No! God makes us realize that in all things He is to be glorified. God had this happen to such an innocent little boy. But, even in times like these when as a Dad it doesn't seem right, thank you, Father, for allowing this to happen so thousands of people can be drawn around one little boy in order to search their own hearts – my own heart, especially.

There were a lot of things that I had to make right with my wife that were tearing our marriage apart. It's unfortunate that it took seeing my son lying on his deathbed for me to realize it. But I thank God for giving us that forgiveness so that I can walk freely with my wife and not have guilt any longer. The glory is to God.

Thank you Lord, for giving us so much support and allowing us to see the sincere love from others. From the bottom of my heart, I sincerely thank each and every one of you for praying and taking the extra effort in planning benefit dinners, setting up trust funds, starting a make a wish foundation, sending all of the beautiful cards and toys for Cole, and much, much support. I can't wait for the day that as a family we can stand before you all with Cole and personally thank each and every one of you. The praise is to God.

Aaron

One of the things that struck me as quite fascinating when I was going back into the journal entries, is that as of August 4 there were 17,000 hits on Cole's website. At the time, I could hardly believe this number was even possible. But six weeks later, it rose to over 550,000 hits. Only by the blessing of God's hand would this be possible, and only by God's divine appointment was the next part of my story possible.

This story is about how God flashed before my eyes what was going on in my life, and came like a punch in the face – a complete wake-up call that hit me like a rock regarding how God brought somebody into my life to change me from the inside out. I can honestly say that it's amazing how God works, but however He does it, who are we to argue about how and why He does anything?

This story is one that comes from the directing hand of God putting all the pieces of the puzzle together, painting that part of the picture in front of my face so I eventually could stand back and see the entire piece of art as a whole. It is a story that prior to these events, I would have been hiding behind the biggest wall so people wouldn't see the real me. For me to include the story in this book can only be done because the power of sin and guilt is no longer hovering over my shoulders. *"If we confess our sins, he is faithful and just to forgive us our sins, and to cleanse us from all unrighteousness." (1 John 1:9)*

I understand that the following events are specific to my life. The events in this testimony may be completely different in context to your personal convictions, but when you look at the entire blanket of sins in our sinful nature, it is all the same. The best part about it is that God is standing with his arms wide open, saying: *"Come unto me, all ye that labor and are heavy laden, and I will give you rest." (Matthew 11:28)* It was I who was heavy laden. For eight years I was hiding behind lies – lies that told me that I was alone and nobody needs to know about my actions – it was my secret.

Fortunately, I was able to find hope and healing through Jesus Christ; the unfortunate thing is that I had to go through the extreme pain of seeing Cole lying on his deathbed before I had the courage to boldly confess the things on my heart. It was then that I realized that I didn't care what anybody thought of me. I was already at the bottom of life. The best part of the story is the fact that I hid behind the lies for eight years and now in a few seconds, that feeling of guilt was lifted instantly. How was this possible? It was only through the grace of God. I hope and pray that if you are hiding behind any walls that are tugging at your conscience or struggling with any relationships, whether it be with your spouse or just a friend, that you will not wait until it is your child or loved one on that deathbed to seek forgiveness. Please realize that today can be the day of grace and salvation.

For years I had a mask hiding the innermost thoughts of my heart. For years I was walking a life that was full of Christianity on the outside and a bitter taste of sin on the inside. So many times I would commit myself to walking a holy and righteous life, commit to praying, reading, and studying, only to fall – trapped in Satan's lies and strong-holds time and time again. What I'm going to talk about is a topic that is more often swept under the rug than brought to light, and that is why I think it's time to make a stand.

It was Saturday, August 2, when we were in the Pediatrics Intensive Care Unit (PICU) of the hospital when someone came to our room to tell us that we had some visitors. We didn't think much of it since we often had more visitors at the hospital than I think we ever had at home. Many of them were local residents who wanted to stop in and say "hi" and see how Cole was doing. We were told that it was our sister-in-law, Honey, from South Carolina, with some friends. Her friends hardly knew each other – they were strangers who became brothers and sisters through faith around this one common thread that was Cole. Honey began telling us about a pastor she had come in contact with over the last few days. He somehow heard about Cole and was in prayer for him. He explained how the Lord laid Cole upon his heart and that he needed to pray for him and visit him in the hospital. The next thing we knew, this pastor, who came from Georgia to Wisconsin to meet Cole and pray with him, was here at the hospital. Keep in mind that he had absolutely no ties to any of our family and had not even heard about Cole until a few days prior to his arrival in Marshfield.

Moireen and I immediately had thoughts and concerns about this man as to who he was and what he stood for. We wanted to know if it was right to allow a complete stranger to come in and pray over Cole. We could not imagine the thoughts going through the pastor's mind at this time as he had come all the way from Georgia to be with Cole, and we had essentially closed the doors to him. He was answering a call and was probably feeling rejected. I remember his humbleness and stewardship and thought if it was meant to be, the Lord would still open the door. Meanwhile, our guard was still up and our visitors were on their way out. Without any knowledge of the visitors, Moireen and I went to find the pastor in order to speak with him and get to know him better.

I would call this God's timing. We wanted to get information about the pastor and his background, his beliefs, and why he felt compelled to come to Wisconsin to be with us. The pastor explained how the Lord had laid Cole upon his heart. He said that this was much bigger than just for Cole. In his mind it was the beginning of a revival. It was for all of us. He said there is a generation of curses that needs to be broken, particularly in the churches of America as a whole, but starting with us.

Suddenly my wife broke down crying, almost to the point that it was uncontrollable, and she was hardly able to stand. Instantly I had this overwhelming feeling of guilt and shame. The things that I had been hiding for years had to come out. There was no denying that this was the time to make everything right with my wife.

Less than thirty seconds earlier, my comfort of hiding behind that wall was still there. The wall was still standing, but now it had to be brought down. It wasn't something that could happen block by block – it was much bigger than that. This wall was going to crash – there was nothing I could do to stop it. With the thought of Cole lying on his deathbed and suddenly realizing what life is worth living for, it was no wonder that the wall was coming down as if a bomb had been planted next to the foundation. God was speaking to my heart in a way that I never felt before. It was a moment that God had planned from the start in order for me to get my life back together. I came to the immediate conclusion that God knew what it would take for me to see the light. He knew that the love I had for my son was more than any love I had for anyone – even more than the love I had for my wife, I was ashamed to admit. It was my wake-up call, and I had nothing to do with the planning of this occurrence. I began telling my wife everything that I had on my heart and that I had been keeping from her for all of these years.

What I had kept from her were things of which I was not proud. They were things that I considered to be my own personal secrets and the devil kept telling me were "no big deal." Little did I understand how big of a deal they were. There were things that have been on my back for years, acts that the little bird inside of me called my conscience would never let me forget, and that I wanted to brush under the rug, but the rug never seemed large enough. It always would be that I would tell Moireen the few things that did not seem to fit under the rug. The small items that the rug would not cover and what I thought were not a big deal would be brought to light, while the big problems seemed to stay hidden.

The rug was covering a multitude of things that all dealt with sexual integrity, a topic that I know is a huge problem in the world, but more importantly, in the future of churches across America. It's a problem of gigantic proportion, a problem that for me started when I was a young person in middle school. It was a time that may have lasted an hour but scarred my mind with images that would last a lifetime.

We were at a friend's home for a sleepover when one of the kids thought it would be cool to watch a pornographic movie. It was the moment my innocence was broken and my entire life would be affected in some shape or form. It was an experience that the devil helped me brush under the rug. Unfortunately it worked, for a while, until again the bird on my shoulder got the better of me.

Two years later my life took another turn when an upperclassman suddenly committed suicide. That hit me directly in the heart because I walked by that boy in the halls daily and I always saw him alone. I never did speak to him or even as much as try to be friends with him. A few days after his funeral, there was a youth weekend at one of the churches. I remember sobbing in one of the pews, giving my life to the Lord for His Glory. I was on an emotional high from which it was hard to be torn down.

It just so happened that I had planned to go on a mission trip shortly with a group from our church. This had been planned for months and fell on the week after I gave my life to the Lord. I was off to the country of Guatemala for seven days to help restore a church with which we are affiliated. Not only was the church restored, but my heart was not far behind.

One of the things that hit me the hardest when I was in Guatemala was how the families had absolutely nothing to their name or stature – nothing that guaranteed them anything in the future – no 401(k) plans, retirement benefits, pensions – nothing. Yet, they seemed to be the happiest people you could ever meet. They were just happy to have the opportunity to listen to the Word of God. It felt like it was such a blessing to be able to be even a small part of that ministry.

After I returned, I was on fire for the Lord, committed to His calling. I would find myself in church every Sunday, trying to walk a life that would glorify God. But eventually my zeal would burn down to ashes, just like any fire will do. Before I knew what was happening, Satan was slowly bringing me back to a life that kept God on the outside and Aaron on the inside. One of the ways that I felt God was on the outside was because there were again times that I was all alone – trapped, lonely, and falling into the snares of the devil. It was through the Internet that my curiosity would get the best of me. It was amazing how the devil worked during that time. It was always when I was alone that mysteriously a dumb pop-up of a certain advertisement or picture would show up. I knew that it had to be of Satan because the pop-up never appeared when I was around others or in public. It was always in a place where I was alone.

Thinking that there would be no one around to watch me or know what I was getting into, my mind kept telling me that it was okay – only this once, and how could one time ever affect anything. It's okay – nobody needs to know. The thoughts kept racing through my head that I'm only looking. It's not like I would ever do anything or cheat on someone. It escalated from one time to several times, at first a glance, then to gawking. It was something that would not go away.

My high school years went by and pornography was never something I looked at on a regular basis. That is how I justified it. I wasn't addicted. How could I be? It was all under control. Besides, when I get married, all of these thoughts and desires will just disappear. It was always being justified by something else. During this whole time, I was still being the normal, everyday church boy attending the youth group. I would never say that I didn't have the Holy Spirit working in me at the time. I did. It seemed like I was always at the altar rail confessing my sins and hearing my sins forgiven. It's just that the devil kept lying to me and telling me that there was no problem and it was okay... it's only a time here and a time there. Meanwhile I was constantly being convicted, especially immediately following the act. I would tell myself that this wouldn't happen again, only to find myself in the same position later. Then things began to get worse. The devil is sly and realizes that he has much better luck luring us little by little. That's exactly what he did with me. He convinced me that it would be okay if I kissed another girl while dating someone else. Besides, it's only a kiss. That first kiss with someone else felt so wrong, but before long it didn't feel so wrong. Meanwhile, after the kiss was conquered, it now was okay to experiment further. As long as I didn't have sex with a girl, I reasoned it was okay.

Suddenly it was brought to the next level without my even knowing it. Needless to say, I would continue to tell myself that all of this would just stop once I got married. I would tell myself that this was okay and that nobody needed to know. It wasn't long before my conscience got the best of me and I had to tell my girlfriend that I cheated on her. The only problem was that I wasn't completely honest with her. I found myself in one white lie that turned into one covering that lie, and so on. I guess I was just afraid to tell her the whole truth – afraid and nervous as to what she would think of me. I thought that in keeping some of it secret, it would be okay, and maybe then she wouldn't break up with me. For some reason that lie stuck with me for years to follow. Years later I would find myself continuing to lie to cover up the truth.

That girl who I was dating eventually became my bride. All those images that were in my mind would have to stay with me into marriage; she was the bride that even though she won my physical virginity, had lost my mental and psychological virginity years prior.

Remember the promises that I had made earlier, the promises that all this would suddenly end at marriage? We were years into our marriage, and there I was back on the Internet into the same pile of garbage I was into years ago. This time I got caught in a lie as she discovered my addiction to pornography. I never wanted to admit it was an addiction until I realized that addiction by definition is deciding not to do something and finding yourself not only doing it, but getting worse. I saw the thing many would call the "creep" happening before my very eyes. I confessed to her that I had problems but continued to tell myself it was not an addiction. Also, I did not tell her all of it. I would always sugar-coat the disgusting parts, again finding myself trapped in more lies. Needless to say, it didn't end with marriage. My lies had continued, and they weren't getting any easier. I had hidden behind them for many years – now the walls were coming down.

As I began to tell Moireen everything, the walls were being shattered all around me. All of these lies that I had been covering up were finally made right. It was something I wanted to do for years, but I had been so afraid, wondering what she might think of me. I thought that it would be so hard to do. Let me tell you, all I can say is: "Why in the world did I not do that from the beginning?" If I had only told her the truth from the beginning, I wouldn't have had to admit to years of lies. It was such a release and it made me feel so free. After hiding it for almost eight years, I could finally walk free – free to admit who I was to my wife, free to walk with her without guilt or shame, and free of being afraid. I was instantly transformed into a new person. I did not care what people would think of me or who I was.

Do you think I would feel comfortable sharing this if I didn't feel free? God allowed Moireen to have compassion upon me so that I could hear all my sins were forgiven and washed in the sea of grace. It was finally over. God knew what it would take for me to come to grips with reality and myself. He knew that I loved Cole more than anyone else and I would do anything for him, particularly when he was on his deathbed. It didn't matter at that point if people cared or how people would look upon my past or me. It was all about Cole. Nothing else mattered, and for that I can do nothing else but PRAISE GOD.

A pastor later told me of an analogy that I want to share with all of you. It's an analogy that was so fitting, and I saw it happen in my life. He said that when we are married, we have a covenant between God and our spouse, a covenant that is represented in the form of a wedding ring. The ring forms a circle, a circle whose purpose is to form walls against the devil and his angels in our marriage. We have to be so careful that we don't let Satan grasp even a sliver of that ring. When he starts out in a small way, no matter how innocent it may feel, he gets us to open that covenant between God and our spouse that will allow him to enter in and destroy the marriage. All it takes is the smallest sliver to allow one more sliver to be taken, and eventually enough that he has a strong hold on our marriage without our even knowing or understanding. We have to be careful.

I struggled writing this trying to determine how much detail and depth I should go into on the topic of sexual integrity among men and teenagers across the country and particularly in the American churches. There are more details and topics that could be discussed in great length about this, but I do not want to take away from Cole's story. I just wanted to touch upon what was laid upon my heart, because I know that so many men are having the same struggles I had. I just felt that it's time to take a stand in our world and crush the enemy, send him back to where he belongs, not in our families and churches.

If you are in a dating relationship, please learn from my mistakes. Don't follow in my footsteps, as I was ashamed and scared to admit who I was and what I had done. You see, that's where all of this had started. You know how it is when you start dating someone when you go over the entire Question and Answer thing from the beginning. Guess what? That Q&A portion of our dating relationship was where I first began getting myself into trouble. It was then that I was embarrassed of who I was. At that time, I didn't want to do anything to potentially ruin the opportunity I had to date this beautiful girl, whom I absolutely adored.

When it was my turn to talk about the past, I decided that it would be better if I didn't tell her everything. Maybe then I would make myself look better and secure this opportunity. Well, now I can look back and only offer advice to others that this was absolutely the WRONG approach. It was the first lie that began building a wall between us in our relationship. From that moment on, I had to always be careful as to what I would say to maintain the initial lie. It was a single lie that turned into a sea of frustration and secrets. Now I had my own secret from her that I could keep hidden in a storage space for all of the future secrets to hide.

The story goes on to eventually winning the heart of the girl I was chasing at the time – it was Moireen. I had won her heart initially, but for the next eight years I lost her true heart. Think about this for a minute. If I had been a real man and admitted to her who I really was from the start, it would have given me the perfect picture of who she was as a young woman of faith; I would have seen how she would have dealt with past mistakes. Would she have forgiveness towards me? Would she dump me because of who I was? If so, then maybe I should have considered why I was with her. Knowing her heart now, I could have found out from day one that she did have a heart of forgiveness and compassion.

I guess the moral of this story for those who are in this position today is to just be real. Make that choice to be a real man or woman and confess the things that we have done in the past. If the person that you are in a relationship with can't see past who you were, then I'm sorry to burst your bubble but you really need to examine why you are in that relationship.

I can tell you from experience, and any other married couple could also tell you, that when you're married, there WILL be times that you need your spouse to have the power of forgiveness upon you. We fail daily, and that is why it is essential to have that open relationship with your spouse. Please take advice from someone who had to be crushed and torn from the inside out. You have the opportunity to learn from my mistakes – please take advantage of the lessons I had to learn the hard way.

Forty-seven percent of Christians in America admit that pornography is a major problem in their homes (From: *Internet Filter Review, Pornography Statistics 2003*), and those are only the ones who admit that it is a serious problem.

Many of these men have given up confessing this sin and asking God's forgiveness. After hundreds or even thousands of times of acting out (again), feeling guilty and remorseful (again), making even stronger commitments to live in purity (again), only to fail (again), they are discouraged and are giving up (From: *First Steps, National Coalition for the Protection of Children and Families.*).

Do you realize that pornography is a bigger business in the United States than major league baseball, professional football, and basketball combined? Statistics reveal that Americans spend more than one billion dollars per month on pornography and sexually oriented businesses. I could almost guarantee that most people have never heard these statistics before. It's no wonder why it is all kept quiet and very few choose to talk about it when there is so much money to be made. (From: *Battling the Storm, National Coalition for the Protection of Children and Families.*)

Small group therapy sessions are important in understanding the noose of sexual addiction. **But the cross of Christ is the only thing that can set us free.** *(Pure Desire, page 88, by Ted Roberts.)*

* * * * * * *

The preceding testimony is a part of the story where I came to realize that God had a very specific and divine appointment for me that day when the pastor from Georgia visited us at the hospital. It was an appointment that was designed to use this man from across the country to help facilitate a meeting with my wife, but more importantly, my meeting with God.

Chapter 7

Count Your Many Blessings

Thursday, August 7, 2008, 1:22 p.m.

Cole's breathing tube was extracted at 9:30 p.m. Wednesday night. The good news is that he is breathing as the doctor expected – faster, but okay. The not so good news is that his pain seems to be back as bad as it was before he was incubated. We have a little dilemma because all of the pain medicines are also respiratory depressants (they will affect his breathing, which has been monitored so closely). The doctors are trying to find the happy medium between his pain and breathing.

I'm beginning to think that the only words in Cole's vocabulary are Mommy, Daddy, and "tummy hurts." There is nothing worse than when he looks you in the face and says, "Mommy, Daddy, HELP; my tummy hurts." What can you do or say to that? Please continue to pray for a miracle for this amazing little man. I will continue to keep you all updated more frequently now that he is fully awake. Until then, let's keep storming the heavens with our prayers. Thank you and God Bless

Aaron

Friday, August 8, 2008, 4:16 p.m.

Another day passed with our hearts aching. Cole's pain just doesn't seem to want to go away, much the same as yesterday with the "owies" and "tummy hurts." However, today we had one moment that I will always cherish. It was something so simple that most of us would probably laugh and think that we were silly if I told you how excited we were about a smile. How often do we get excited when we watch our kids smile, laugh, play, or have fun? Well, today Cole "smiled" for the first time in a week; wow, what an amazing feeling. The story is so cute that I have to share it.

I was lying next to Cole, and of course we fell asleep. When we woke up, I whispered to Cole, "I have to get out of the bed and use the bathroom before I wet my pants." I didn't even think that Cole was listening, but then I heard him chuckle. I jumped out of bed and grabbed my camera. Luckily he held a smile long enough that I was able to capture a Kodak moment. The picture will be posted for all to enjoy. One cannot underestimate the power of a smile. That single smile is a ray of sunshine on this dark day for Moireen and me.

Aaron

As the journal stated, let's not underestimate the power of a smile. Before Cole got sick a little over three weeks ago, he had been a child who was always smiling. Like most kids, he had a smile that would immediately cover a multitude of our frustrations and irritations. At times, it even felt like we couldn't punish him, until we realized that we still had to be parents. I will always remember the morning Cole held that smile long enough for me to get out of bed and take a picture. For those of you who knew Cole, you would soon realize that he got comfort from rubbing his ear lobe. All I can remember about that morning is his smile from cheek to cheek and his hand rubbing his ear lobe.

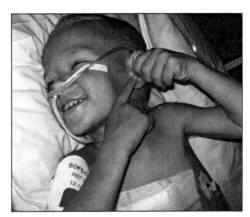

First Kodak smile in weeks

The preciousness of that smile was like the e-mail I recently received from one of Cole's many admirers. It was a story about a mother who was awakened one night by her daughter crawling into her bed to snuggle with her for comfort. She went on to say that her daughter began rubbing her head, but the daughter was the one doing the comforting, not her. Her mind suddenly was filled with thoughts of having to get up in a few hours to get ready for work. But more importantly, she stated how she couldn't help but think how much Moireen and I would want to have the opportunity to have Cole snuggle with us.

A simple time of snuggling can change our thoughts from, "this child is ruining my precious sleep," to "here is an intimate moment that will forever be etched in my heart." Of course, this all comes in moderation because we have to still remember that we are called to be parents at the same time. But the thought is still there. If we could only change our mindset in life, we would be a lot better off. It's the same theory as the question, "Is your glass half empty or is it half full?"

At the beginning of this book, I mentioned how I had hurt my back in hitting a drive when I was golfing in South Carolina. Well, here's a story that perfectly describes Cole's "heart" condition during his days undergoing treatment. My wife and I would often snuggle in the hospital bed beside Cole. This particular time it was my turn. For some odd reason, it was embedded in Cole's mind that Dad had hurt his back.

Now I hate to admit it, but I was the biggest baby regarding my sore back on our way back from that trip. Yes, it did hurt, but Cole even remembered my hurting back one month later. I obviously talked too much about it and evidently complained when sitting up in the bed.

Cole looked over at me and said, "Daddy, your back still hurt?" Then to top if off, he reached over with his weak and tired arms and started to rub my lower back in the exact spot that was injured. Again, it was just one of those moments that made me realize how big his heart was. He was literally tied up with the tubes and wires, battling for his life, but rather than pitying himself, he was comforting his big, complaining Dad.

Saturday, August 9, 2008, 7:28 p.m.

The doctor came to visit today. He did not have a whole lot of good news for us concerning Cole's pain. It appears that his pain is being caused by the mass of the tumor. Unfortunately, until the tumor starts being attacked by the chemo, our hearts will be torn apart watching him. Cole's system is getting more immune to the fentanyl. The doctor said that if he gave the same dosage to anybody else cold turkey, it would knock them out. We can only sit and continue to pray. The Bible says that we should make our requests known to God. I believe we are all doing that now. Continue to pray for a miracle for Cole and his pain. I hope that none of you have to go through this.

Aaron

I have never encountered anything worse than seeing my son in so much pain. But worst of all, was having the doctors tell us there was nothing they could do. That's exactly what was happening with Cole. For weeks we were in his room with our hands tied behind our backs. There was nothing that we could do.

The tumor was continuing to grow in his abdomen and pushing on organs, causing an enormous amount of pain and discomfort. The last definite measurement of the tumor was 6" x 4". We would soon find out that those measurements would only be a wish. Cole's body was becoming intolerant to the pain medicine. Everything they tried was only as good as the writing on its label. It didn't matter what they prescribed, it wasn't working.

It's hard to explain how it felt to sit in that hospital room, knowing that your son has this horrible disease attacking his body. The only hope we had was in the drugs they were pumping into his body now, or had pumped in through the chemotherapy that ended a few days earlier.

It didn't take long to realize that there was a more powerful place in which we should put our trust and confidence, and that place was with our Lord God Himself. We realized that it was God who would be our only true hope for strength, comfort, peace, and understanding. Before long, the doctors would switch off Cole's pain meds to try some different drugs, which only helped temporarily.

Tuesday, August 12, 2008, 11:22 p.m.

Hi everybody. Today was a little better than those of the past. There were lots of visitors, a change in the pain medication (which seemed to help a little), and Cole was begging for more toys. It's so exciting to actually see him want things in his hands. The worst part, however, is when you can tell that he wants to get up and walk, or go to the playroom, or just sit on your lap. But yet he is restricted by severe abdominal discomfort and what seems to be like hundreds of wires and monitors hooked up to him. It is cute when he collects his toy airplanes. It's almost like he tries to see how many he can hold in one hand. I must confess I'm impressed. I counted nine being held by his tiny, little fingers. Anyway, it is exciting to see him at least want toys again.

Cole seems to be losing a lot of weight due to lying in that bed for two weeks. His arms especially seem to be fading away, but his belly doesn't want to decrease in size at all. It holds steady at 64 centimeters. Because of the change in drugs, the doctors didn't want to release him back to PEDS (pediatrics) yet, but hopefully tomorrow.

The doctor is hoping to get a CT scan done a little earlier than what was last expected. They think that our best hope is to get the tumor removed surgically, as long as it is free from the aorta. I was reading about this disease today and realized that instead of being one in a million in all kids, they claim one in a million of all cancer patients, which is 0.2% of all cancer patients. However, in Brazil it is said to be 10% of all cancer patients. Why is it higher there? No one knows just yet. But anyway, enough of the senseless numbers – our God is greater than any number.

Thanks for the continual prayers. I pray that God will use this so Cole can be a living testimony that He is alive and true. But more importantly, that God can be glorified through this. I want to say thank you to all who have shown your love to the other patients that we have been connected with through CaringBridge. I was amazed when I checked with Jacob's site on how many of you had already answered the call to show God's love to those you meet and with whom you come in contact. I want to leave you with another CaringBridge site where I hope you can offer some support. We meet here in the PICU, and we now call them our new neighbors. But they are in need of prayer and support, so please encourage and uplift them. Good night and God bless!

Aaron

Wednesday, August 13, 2008, 12:13 p.m.

It always seems like I post some good news about Cole and then we will get some bad news. So here it is. Last night his breathing went sour again. It was probably because of the pain meds and extra fluid in his body. This morning they shut off all the fluids entering his body orally, and now it's all given through the Hickman line. They took some x-rays this morning and found more junk in his lungs than before. At this point, they are not sure if it is more tumors or excess fluid. The doctors are starting to consider surgery on the tumors. Apparently that seems to be our best hope.

I will let you know as soon as we get more information. Thanks.

Aaron

What I experienced in those last two days was that Cole's life was a constant roller coaster of emotions in us. You would go up, and then back down, over and over again. The same holds true in life but maybe through a bigger picture and time frame. One day we can be on an emotional or spiritual high, and before we know it, we are back in the valleys of life. Somebody once told me that a mountain never has a sheer cliff all the way to the top. It always has ups and downs, some ups are bigger than the downs and some downs are larger and longer than the ups. Eventually the end would always lead to the top. Isn't that true in life? The only difference is that the "top" would eventually be "heaven," and we all have to make the decision of whether or not to climb that mountain, taking the road that is less traveled.

The best part of this is that it is not some great revelation by me, but it is a promise given to us by God. The scripture says there is a time for everything. Ecclesiastes 3:1, 2, 4: *"To every thing there is a season, and a time to every purpose under the heaven: A time to be born, and a time to die; a time to weep, and a time to laugh; a time to mourn, and a time to dance."*

When we talk about making the decision of whether or not we want to walk down the road less traveled and overcome the ups and downs of the mountain of life, I would like to leave you with a quote from Matthew 16:26: *"For what is a man profited, if he shall gain the whole world, and lose his own soul? Or what shall a man give in exchange for his soul?"*

Wednesday, August 13, 2008, 10:58 p.m.

The doctor came to visit today to talk about the next steps. It sounds like we are scheduled to do another important CT scan on Friday morning. The results of that scan will be sent to the surgeons at The Children's Hospital in Milwaukee. If the surgeons feel confident that they can remove some of the tumors, we will be going to Milwaukee for the surgery. However, for now we can just continue to pray for healing. The most important tumor that they are monitoring is the tumor in the IVC. Currently, it is blocking some of the blood flow to the heart. As soon as we hear more, we will let you know.

When we were in the PEDS at the beginning of our stay, we met a very special little boy who truly cared about Cole before they even met. His name is Matt, and his mother told us that when he heard Cole crying in the room next door, he wanted to get out of bed and give Cole a hug. WOW, the heart of a child! Matt has leukemia and also Down's syndrome. Now his kidneys are beginning to fail. It would really mean a lot to him if we could all visit his site to encourage him. His 12th birthday is tomorrow, so please drop a note to him and his family at: www.caringbridge. org/visit/mattpliska.

Aaron

Thursday, August 14, 2008, 6:41 p.m.

The CT scan has been postponed until Monday. They felt that it would be better if it was done closer to the date of the surgery. It appears we will get transferred to Milwaukee in the middle of next week. The surgeons feel they will be able to perform surgery on a few of the tumors on August

25. *However, the surgeon will contact us to see if we are okay with some of the extreme risks involved.*

We have been absolutely amazed at how many people have shown their support for Cole through CaringBridge, cards, benefits, and the community. We have had many visitors, many whom we have never met before. Today we had a couple from Hurley, WI stop in to show their support and love toward Cole. If Cole could only know how many lives are being touched by his struggles.

I was reading one of the guestbook entries where it was written that their lives have been touched in many different ways through Cole. Praise God!!! Some friends were visiting when the comment was made about Cole's skinned knees (a typical boy thing). How many times as parents do we look at skinned knees, bumps, and bruises as a bad thing? What I would give right now to see Cole just get a bump, and a bruise would be nothing short of a miracle. The next time you see a child with a skinned knee, you can praise God for their health and the ability to even be able to play.

Just stop and thank God for the blessings that He has given, like the following song says:

WHEN UPON LIFE'S BILLOWS

When upon life's billows you are tempest-tossed,
When you are discouraged, thinking all is lost
Count your many blessings, name them one by one,
And it will surprise you what the Lord hath done.

Refrain:
Count your blessings, name them one by one;
Count your blessings, see what God hath done;
Count your blessings, name them one by one;
Count your many blessings, see what God hath done.

Are you ever burdened with a load of care?
Does the cross seem heavy you are called to bear?
Count your many blessings, every doubt will fly,
And you will be singing as the days go by.

When you look at others with their lands and gold,
Think that Christ has promised you His wealth
    untold;
Count your many blessings, money cannot buy,
Your reward in heaven, nor your home on high.

So, amid the conflict, whether great or small,
Do not be discouraged, God is over all;
Count your many blessings, angels will attend,
Help and comfort give you to your journey's end.

– Johnson Oatman

It's times like these that songs come to mind. God truly is amazing. My wife and I again thank you for your support. When we hear about the things that are going on in the community for Cole, it really makes us proud of our city, especially of the special people that make our community what it is. Thanks be to God for all of you.
We read the guestbook again and saw entries from many states: Hawaii, Tennessee, Washington, the Carolina's, Florida – and many more. It's just another reminder to us that God is alive and real. Until next time, take care.

Aaron and Moireen

___

If there was ever a time that somebody would ask me to try to explain Cole, the next journal entry would most certainly be the one that I would share with everybody. It's the true heart of Cole, and I honestly think it would probably hold true for most kids. If we as adults would only take a minute or two to learn from these children, we all would be a lot better off in this life. As I am writing this, my daughter, Chaneille, just woke up from her nap and came running down the long hall to give Dad a hug. She was smiling all the way. I didn't ask for a hug; it's just the heart of a child. Maybe I should take some lessons?

Sunday, August 17, 2008, 10:11 p.m.

After what I would call a horrible day for Cole, one which I would compare to his worst day yet, I am not able to do anything else but think about tomorrow and the CT scan. Cole was lying there kicking his feet in pain and crying about his "tummy." His abdominal girth was bigger today than any other day. The only thing that got me through lying next to him during all of this was that God must really be working inside of this little man.

During Cole's pain today, his sister was in the room. At one point she started crying while she was lying with Mom and Cole. He took one of Chaneille's hands and with his other hand, stroked her face with his fingers and said to her, "It's okay, Chaneille... it's okay," and continued to hold her hand. This was amazing to me. It's enough to make a grown man cry. A little later he reached up to her and gave her a big bear hug and kiss – a little boy who is going through so much, but yet upholds his duty as a big brother. What an example to all of us! This reminds me of why a little boy in China turned back to save a few others when his school building collapsed in an earthquake earlier this year. A reporter asked, "what made you turn back to get your friends?" His response was, "I was class leader that day! It was my duty!!" What a lesson for all of us with responsibilities. Sometimes it takes kids to show us.

The CT scan tomorrow is going to tell a lot of stories, the biggest of which will be whether or not the surgeons are going to feel comfortable about performing the surgery. As soon as we hear anything, we will be sure to let all of you know. Let's pray that the news will be good.

Aaron

08/17/2008 18:32

Cole loving his sister Chaneille

Finally the long wait was over. After the first round of chemo, we would soon find out how the tumor responded. The doctors' hopes were that the tumor would have shrunk as well as the masses in Cole's lungs. With chemo being our only hope as far as medicines were concerned, we could only hope that it had attacked the tumor and masses. We didn't expect that this would be the day when we would receive the most devastating news to date. It proved to be a perfect example of one of the valleys that would be a lot longer and deeper than others we had faced.

Monday, August 18, 2008, 1:22 p.m.

"Lord, hear our cry!! Why?? Why the pain, why the suffering? Lord why is Cole only getting worse? You know all things, Lord... Please comfort him. Give him peace. If it is meant that you take him, Lord, please do so soon."

The result of the CT scan was not what we wanted to hear. The tumor in his IVC has grown significantly to disrupt the blood flow to his heart. The masses have filled his lungs from 10% coverage to what is now about 75%; the tumor in the liver has also grown. "Please, Lord, help us! Give us strength, Lord. You know that we are about at the bottom of our ability to cope with this disease, so please help."

We are not sure of any surgeries, as yet. We hope to meet with the doctor later this afternoon.

Aaron

Not only did the chemotherapy not work in fighting the disease, it almost acted like it fed it. With the tumors growing, Cole never ceased to amaze us. Although the following journal entry had nothing to do with trying to improve Cole's physical condition, it had everything to do with my personal feelings for his condition. I wondered if he would still have the same sense of humor and character. If there ever was a time that he gave me assurance that through it all he still was the same Cole, this was it.

Tuesday, August 19, 2008, 5:40 p.m.

What started out to be a disappointing day turned into an absolute blessing with Cole entertaining us in spite of his pain. It all started early in the early morning when we got a call that he wanted to see us. When I went to see him, he was wide awake and waiting for me. He had some screams for the nurse, but managed to soon calm down.

Cole had very dry feet and hands so I asked him if he wanted me to rub some lotion on them. He was okay with that, and it wasn't long until he was rubbing the lotion on my hands also. He must have thought my hands were dry because he rubbed them for about fifteen minutes, and I enjoyed every minute of it. A few hours later, he asked for some ice. As I was holding the cup of ice for him, occasionally some ice would drop out. When I picked up the ice and missed throwing it into the garbage, he would say, "That's all right, Daddy." It might not sound like much, but I have to tell you that was AWESOME!

He still had a lot of pain today, but it just seems like every day he gives us a brief moment of excitement. This afternoon he wanted to get out of bed and explore the hallways, patio, and playroom. He didn't really do a whole lot other than sit in my lap, but he did get a little excited when we saw the fish tank and visited the patio. All we can do is thank God for the time we shared.

The plans to be transported to Milwaukee are delayed until a bed opens up for Cole. However, the delay doesn't really affect the time for the surgery. The surgeons still haven't given us the details of the surgery. Thanks for the prayers and support; it is so much appreciated. It was an awesome turnout for the benefit dinner, everybody. I have heard a lot of good news about the volunteers that helped. I will thank you all personally some day, but for now, "thank you."

Aaron

Wednesday, August 20, 2008, 7:51 a.m.

The transfer to Milwaukee is finally official, and we'll be leaving in about an hour. We pray for safe travels, and we will surely miss Marshfield. For all the nurses that may be reading this, I just want you all to know that everybody did an AWESOME job with Cole. He told his nurse, Heather, and me that he did not want to leave.

Thank you all for making our stay so comfortable. We will be back to visit again. Maybe Cole will be more like himself next time so that he can give you all hugs. Bye for now.

Aaron

From CaringBridge Readers

The very week I was asked to pray for Cole, my marriage seemed to be questionable. Cole's story gave me strength, courage and faith – the reminder of what God can do, all that I have in this life, and where my focus should lie. We are now working on our marriage – cherishing the blessings we have, reminding ourselves how short life is, and being thankful for the normal and average days. Cole's life helped save my marriage.

– From Wisconsin

Despite having a weak stomach, I have been following CaringBridge stories for quite a few years now. We lost a little boy at three weeks of age due to a cord injury at birth, and our almost seven-year-old has an immune deficiency and has had pneumonia 19 times. We almost lost him when he was two weeks old.

This has brought me to the "CaringBridge life," and it is why I have followed and supported Caring-Bridge kids and families for years. I have never seen such a huge response as I have seen to Cole's CaringBridge site, a little boy from our own congregation! He is a little boy whom I loved to see on Sundays, with a big grin on his face and a twinkle in his eye – a little boy who is a shirt-tail relative of my husband. God has worked in my life through Aaron and Moireen's trial with Cole. I am in awe of God and how He, through one little boy, who couldn't go to a seminary and couldn't memorize scripture (or even read it, for that matter), spoke many sermons.

– From Michigan

Chapter 8

Preparing for Surgery

It was a long day transferring to Milwaukee, but everything turned out very well, despite our delays. We were scheduled to leave Marshfield around 9:00 a.m., but didn't actually leave until the afternoon. It couldn't be helped since the Life Flight helicopter was busy all morning. They actually sent a plane that originated in Chicago, stopped to pick up the transport team in Milwaukee, and then picked up Cole. Being delayed, we worried whether we were going to go at all that day, but the transfer was made successfully. It was a long three-hour drive from Marshfield to Milwaukee for my wife and me.

Thursday, August 21, 2008, 12:22 p.m.

Cole is scheduled for surgery at 8:00 a.m. Friday morning. We just left a meeting with the surgeons and doctors. The surgery is going to be very dangerous and involves the removal of the mass in his abdomen and attempts to remove the tumor in the IVC. It is expected to take anywhere from 8 to 12 hours, depending on what they find when he is opened up. This is not a cure-all surgery.

Afterward they will still have a lot of tumor to deal with in his liver and primarily in his lungs. The best way I can describe his lungs is if you would fill a small jar with different sized rocks, and the rocks touch each other. The rocks represent the tumors.

The doctors have told us that without any surgery on some of the tumors, there is a zero chance of survival. I guess we can take the surgery as an answer to prayer.

Tomorrow will be a very big day for Cole. Many people have said if there was anything they could do, to just ask. So here goes. I pray that someone would take the initiative to start blocks of prayer time at 15-minute intervals throughout the day starting at 8:00 a.m. I'm sure that we could find 48 people to have continuous prayer for the surgeons, for Cole, and for his family and friends. If someone would do that for us, it would be amazing.

I'm not sure what would be the easiest way to organize this prayer activity, maybe through a phone number where people could call and be assigned a time to pray. Regardless, may we call upon the Lord for His strength and that His will WILL be done. Cole's current condition is much the same as before. They have again increased his pain meds, and it appears to help. The amount of pain medication he is on is high enough to stop his breathing at any time. However, Cole is still fighting and holding on. Praise God! We will keep you updated as time goes on.

Aaron and Moireen

We arrived at the hospital, said "hi" to Cole, and were quickly taken to a meeting with the surgery team. At that time it was all just a dream, thinking that it wasn't even possible to remove this huge mass in his abdomen – the mass that we saw Cole struggle in pain with for several weeks. It was a major answer to prayer that the surgery was going to happen. Despite the strong efforts of the doctors warning us about how dangerous this surgery was, my emotions were getting the upper hand. The excitement about surgery was overpowering, and I was thinking that this might be the step that he needed to take toward recovery. Everything that we had been hoping for was actually going to come true.

The one thing that I hadn't been thinking about was the fact that Cole had a major tumor in his lungs. My mind was telling me that as soon as they could remove the mass, then the chemotherapy would have a much better chance of working. That's exactly what the doctors were hoping for, as well. We would be working against the clock, trying to get Cole back on the chemotherapy before the tumors in his lungs would have much chance to continue growing. After watching the tumors for four weeks and seeing how they progressed in what seemed like daily leaps and bounds, we soon would know how important each and every day would be.

Friday, August 22, 2008, 1:09 a.m. (PDT)

"Then all the believers were united as they lifted their voices in prayer... give your servants great boldness in their preaching. Send your healing power; may miraculous signs and wonders be done through the name of your holy servant, JESUS." (Acts 4:24a, 29b-30)

My heart is completely overwhelmed reading through the guestbook, receiving e-mails and calls from all of you... people that I have never met, people my family have never met, people we know – everyone has come together for one special three-year-old boy, a little boy who has been enduring more than is imaginable, a little boy, who while in intense pain, brings laughter and joy to his family, a little boy who comforts his Father, Mother, sister, grand-parents, and the rest of the family as he is fighting for his life.

We cannot understand God's ways and often question His thinking at times like this. But something my dear grandma (who just recently went to be with Jesus) has always told me, "Julie, God never promised yellow brick roads or a life without trouble. He has promised us that His ways are the best ways and that He is with us through it all. You see, when you ask the Lord to come into your heart and be your Lord and Savior, He leaves a piece of Himself with us. We are no longer alone but are one with Christ!"

Isn't that such an awesome promise! We can be one with the Living God! For me and my family we put ALL of our hope and trust and faith in Jesus! There is nothing on this earth that is more important than having a personal relationship with Jesus Christ. For it says in the Bible, this life is only a vapor... we need to be ready. We all need to start living each day to its fullest because we are only guar-anteed TODAY! Not tomorrow, just today!

For the people that stepped up instantly to pray and join the prayer vigil, THANK YOU! You heard the need and reacted quickly. That is the most important thing we can do right now. Cole is God's son, and He loves Cole more than we can ever fathom. He knows what's best for Cole. As his family, we are praying for a miracle today, and we BELIEVE that God is still in the business of performing miracles!

Look around you! His miracles are all around us. If you have children sleeping in their beds, that's a miracle! If you have your husband or wife lying next to you, that's a miracle! If you lay your head down and have a roof over your head, that's a miracle! We can count the many bless-ings from our Father, Who loves us more than we can ever know!

Sorry this has been so long. I guess there is just so much on my mind tonight. Again, our families thank you from the bottom of our hearts for everything that everyone has been doing for Cole! You cannot even begin to know the difference that it has made this side of heaven. This is how God designed His church to work. All of you are a part of that church... we praise you Father.

As we soon will begin the prayer vigil, I will close this with a prayer: "Our Father, who art in heaven, Hallowed be Thy name. Thy kingdom come. Thy will be done, in earth as it is in heaven. Give us this day our daily bread, and forgive us our trespasses, as we forgive those who trespass against us. And lead us not into temptation, but deliver us from evil, for Thine is the kingdom, the power, and glory, forever. Amen."

"Dear Daddy in heaven: I praise You for all You have done for us, the blessings that You have given us, the people in our lives, our families, our children, our friends... so many that we have often taken for granted. Lord, I praise You that You have created Cole... You knitted him together in Moireen's womb. You made him perfect because You are the Creator of everything! You are a loving and compassionate Father Who cares so much for His children that when they are in pain, You are in pain. Lord, we are all in pain over this terrible cancer that has invaded Cole's body. Lord, we pray that You would perform a great miracle in a couple of hours as the doctors begin surgery on our little Cole. Thousands are on their knees praying that Your presence would flood that operating room and that Your hands would perform a miracle on Cole! Lord, we ask You for a miracle! We commit him to You, and whatever the outcome, we will still praise You!

"Lord, please be with Aaron, Moireen, Chaneille, Dave, Diane, and everyone else, and pour Your perfect peace over them from the top of their heads to the bottom of their feet.

Help them Lord, as they wait for what would feel like an eternity. We believe in Your entire promises, Lord! Thank You for all that You have done and all that You will do through Your Son, Jesus. Amen." Either Aaron or I will update the journal again as soon as we know more... until then, thank you! Let's flood heaven with prayers.

Cousin Julie

The day of the surgery was one of mixed emotions, knowing it would be a huge step in Cole's progress, but also realizing that all of the realities of the surgery were coming together. Some major difficulties could arise during the surgery considering what they had to do to him and depending on how bad the tumor was in his IVC. The doctors made it very clear that there was a small chance that Cole may not survive the surgery. I recall being in the surgery holding area where parents can say goodbye to their loved one before surgery. All we could do was hug Cole and tell him how much we loved him. We were probably in the room for five to ten minutes, but we both felt like we could have stayed there forever. While in the room, one of the nurses brought a box of tissues for our use.

It was during this time that the concerns of life became absolutely meaningless. It wouldn't have mattered what I had in this life; I would have given it all up for Cole. For the first time I felt what it would feel like to truly want to lay down your life for another. He was my son, only three years old, so innocent, so beautiful, yet he had to be going through this. It just wasn't fair! Why did he have to suffer? How small I felt as a father who was absolutely helpless to do anything for his own son! When he would look straight into my eyes, with tears rolling down his cheeks, there were absolutely no words to describe the insurmountable feelings of hurt, pain, and helplessness that I felt. To see my son, who supposedly was sedated at the time, overcome the sedation, reach up with his arms and give each of us the most comforting, the most difficult, the most beautiful hug we have ever gotten, was heart wrenching. It was as though my heart was literally taken from me; my selfish desires suddenly all vanished. Life seemed to stop. Behind those closed curtains, it felt like the three of us were the only ones alive.

It wasn't easy knowing that Cole knew that something was going to be happening to him. It wasn't fun having our son say good-bye to us and tell us that he loved us. It was supposed to be us as parents doing the comforting and the encouraging in times like this. Not in this case! It was Cole saying his good-byes. Soon after, we were escorted to the waiting room where all we could do was wait, pray, and read the *Caring Bridge* site.

Friday, August 22, 2008, 11:56 a.m.

It's amazing how long a day can be when you're away from the hustle and bustle of everyday life. It feels like we have been in this waiting room for weeks.

One of the latest precious moments we had with Cole was this morning when we were saying "bye" to him before surgery. He was almost completely sedated but he still managed to lift his weak arms and hug us. It was the most touching and emotional hug I have ever experienced.

The cardiac surgeon came to ask us some questions and talk to us. Unfortunately, he had to prepare us for the worst. Although it feels like the surgery decision was a "no brainer," being that the doctors told us that without surgery he has no chance at all, the surgeon wanted to know how aggressive we wanted him to be with the surgery. The extent of the tumor inside his IVC will determine a lot of different things for Cole. If the tumor is as bad as they think it is, it means that Cole could be in the intensive care unit for up to six weeks. He will be very sick afterwards, which means that he will not be able to undergo chemotherapy.

His lung tumor has doubled in size in the past week, so we can only pray for a miracle that his lungs will be able to hold up while recovering from the surgery. The doctors told us that this is a very critical time for Cole. But if God can move mountains and part the Red Sea, He can certainly heal a little boy if it's His will. May God bless you all for your kindness, and may you all feel His presence in your lives.

The nurse just called with the latest update. Everything is going according to plan regarding the surgery. All of Cole's vital signs are good; however, the tumor is extraordinarily large. I should be receiving another update within the next two hours.

Aaron

Friday, August 22, 2008, 3:26 p.m.

We received our update call after 7 1/2 hours of surgery. None of the tumor was removed. It was explained that they have to carefully pry and cut around the perimeter of the tumor to avoid all vital organs. The tumor in the abdomen has to be removed first, and then they can start on the IVC tumor. The IVC surgery is not supposed to take as long because they have a time frame that they must work within. That area of the body is first frozen and the surgery must be done within 45 minutes from the time they start the freeze. If the surgery takes longer, Cole could potentially suffer brain damage.

We were sitting here talking about how valuable relationships in life are. We were thinking about Cole and all of the memories that we have of him: The little things that he always did, the way you could see how he would continue to learn and grow, the way he would run to the window to welcome Dad home. And then from the window, he would run through the breezeway and wait for Mom to open the door. And of course, there were the hugs and kisses. When I sat down, Cole would unlace my work boots and take them off.

My point is that that those memorable events can never be brought back. I wonder how many people take relationships with their kids and/or spouse for granted? If Cole doesn't make it, there will be nothing that will bring him back. If there are marital conflicts or frustrations within families or kids, there is nothing that can bring that person or relationship back once they are gone. I pray that you would make it right while you have the time. The last time that Cole told me, "Daddy, I love you to the moon and back," is so PRICELESS.

Aaron

Friday, August 22, 2008, 5:39 p.m.

The abdominal tumor is OUT. The nurse just came and talked to us. It sounds like Phase 1 of the surgery is done and things went very well. The nurse, Erin, said they had never seen the size and look of such a tumor – it was ugly and the size of a large honeydew melon.

The cardiac team just began their portion of the surgery. They expect to be done about 10:00 p.m. PRAISE GOD!

Aaron

103

Friday, August 22, 2008, 10:22 p.m.

"Lord God, we thank You for Your all knowing and all powerful work that continues to bless our lives through the valleys and when we stand on the mountain top. Lord, we thank You for Your direction with the surgeons and their wisdom and knowledge. Your presence has been felt by all of us Lord, and we thank You for that. We thank You for using Your child as a vessel to proclaim Your Word and unite us all together. Lord, we know that this fight is nowhere near over, but we ask that Your will would be done in Cole's life. We thank You for the successful surgery today. We ask for Your guidance and protection for Cole as we move forward in this battle. We praise Your name to all. In Jesus' name. Amen."

The doctor just met with us and explained that the surgery was a complete success (what a miracle in itself). He told us that although it was long, tedious, and far from over, it could not have gone better. It is now 10:30 p.m. and they expect to have another three hours left and will not be completed until about midnight to 1:00 a.m. Cole's abdomen is still open. He explained that it might not be closed until tomorrow or Monday. I am so happy to give you this praise report. Three weeks ago, the doctor had told us that the cancer was almost completely inoperable because the tumor was literally wrapped around the aorta. Today, thanks to what I believe is an answer to all of your prayers and pleading to God for healing, the tumor was completely removed from around Cole's aorta to only pushing on his aorta. The tumor was able to be removed without the loss of his left kidney. He lost his left adrenal gland, but we shouldn't have to worry about that according to the doctor.

We climbed the first step, but it was a big hurdle for Cole. His lungs are still filled with tumors, so we continue to pray that the chemotherapy and God's healing hand will take care of them. The tumor in the abdomen was about the size of a full-sized football. "LORD, WE THANK YOU FOR THE ANSWERED PRAYERS!!" I wish we could go around to everyone and proclaim that God is alive and real. "Lord, we know that this fight is far from over, but we trust in the fact that You are the same God in the valley as You are on the mountain."

Parents, if you read this yet tonight, I suggest that you go to your children's rooms and thank God for them; not only your children, but more importantly, your spouse. "Thank You, Lord, for life. But more so, we thank You for sending Your Son to die for our sins and the sins of the whole world." Please continue to pray for Cole and... Praise God!!

Aaron and Moireen

Saturday, August 23, 2008, 1:36 a.m.

The surgery is complete. We just greeted Cole with kisses while he was on his way to the PICU to recover. The process took 18 hours, and the surgical team was there throughout this time.

Aaron

What an answer to prayer that everything went so well during the surgery! We had a prayer team constantly praying for its success. It was so awesome to experience the Love of God working within the body of Christ here on earth – the body of believers who banded together around one little boy. It is nothing short of a blessing from God that He was able to take people from every walk of life, many denominations, and many parts of the world and unite them together around Cole. But WHY? I believe God brought something like this about so that people would be brought together in oneness of the Spirit.

It energizes me, but at the same time it frightens me – I wonder if this is all just hype, or will it be something that has the ability to change people for good? It brings me back to that horrible day of 9/11, the day where EVERYONE came together to support our nation, to pray to God, and wonder WHY it happened.

After the events of 9/11, attendance in the American churches immediately increased. Why is it that over time people go back to the same old rut of life? That is the real question, not why did this or that happen, but why is it that something just affects us for a short while? Why isn't it something that brings about REAL change in the lives of people?

I pray for a change that has the ability to save souls and not just fill churches. I pray for a change that starts from the inside and works outward, a change that starts in the heart, and from that brings about a change in character, values, desires, and attitudes.

It is a change that can only happen by knowing the Lord and Savior Jesus Christ as your personal Savior. As it says in Matthew 6:33: *"But seek ye first the kingdom of God and his righteousness; and all these things shall be added unto you."* This is the true change that has the ability to determine where we will spend eternity.

Saturday, August 23, 2008, 4:12 p.m.

I just wanted to let everybody know that as of now, Cole's recovery is going great. "Better than expected so far," the doctor said. Last night before we left him for the night after surgery, I told Cole that Mom and Dad are going to be going to bed. Cole shook his head, NO. Both Grandma and I saw him shake his head, and I asked the nurse if that was possible. She said, "No, he should be completely out." So I asked Cole another question and he answered again. We know he hears us and we know God is hearing us. "Please Lord, continue to work Your healing hand in Cole's life. In Jesus' name, we pray. Amen."

Aaron

I always knew there was something special about Cole, and this was just another one of those times that confirmed it for me. When we were back in the recovery room with him, he answered some of my questions that he should never have been able to answer. It didn't just happen once, but twice, and the nurse was a witness to it. He was supposed to be completely sedated from all of the medicines and drugs given to him for the surgery, a surgery that involved some of the same processes as open-heart surgery. The surgeons had to go through his chest to reach the IVC, and they also had to put him on a by-pass machine.

The fact that he answered my questions with a nod of his head was beyond explanation. The nurse almost laughed at my saying such a

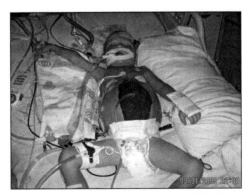

After surgery on August 22nd

thing. I guess Cole wasn't your average three-year-old boy.

From CaringBridge Readers

Cole changed my life indirectly; he has such an impact on your faith. Several weeks ago when my own faith was shaky, I read one of your posts and was immediately humbled and strengthened by your absolute trust in God. It gave me a fresh perspective and instilled a resolve in me to never let go of God and His promises to us. He does answer, not always in the way we'd like Him to, but He does answer. I'm standing on that now and have Cole to thank for it!

– From Florida

I've never met sweet Cole, but his inspiration is so overwhelming and just about impossible to put into words. Cole taught me never to take people for granted, that in a blink of an eye, anything can happen. Cole taught me never to question God's doings and that He has a plan for all of us. Cole taught me that we are in this great big world together and that we all need to stick together and "BE THERE" for each other. Cole taught me not to count the days, but to make the days count. Cole taught me to love a little harder, hug a little longer, smile a little brighter, and to thank God for everything I have. This is the legacy of Cole.

– From Kentucky

Chapter 9

Day by Day

Sunday, August 24, 2008, 10:29 a.m.

Sometimes we don't know why certain people are placed in our lives at certain times. Divine intervention, perhaps. One thing I can tell you is that there have been so many people that I will never meet on this side of heaven that have been there to support us during this time. It's truly such a blessing. I go to Cole's website daily to read the many guestbook entries and see the names of people I might have known but never knew that they cared. Then I see names of people whom I have never met and see that they truly care as well. This is a comfort beyond words.

Cole is doing well but is still very sick. They expect to take him back to surgery on Monday to wash out the inside of his abdomen. If everything goes well enough, they might close his abdomen. He is able to respond at times so we know that he is listening. I will let you know tomorrow how the trip to surgery went. Bye for now.

Aaron

Monday, August 25, 2008, 12:00 noon.

Hello everybody. This has been another busy day for Cole as he goes back to surgery this afternoon for internal cleansing of his abdomen. He seems to be doing well despite having more pain last night. He kept motioning that he has OWIES in his abdomen. It's hard to imagine that he is actually moving around with it being open. It's no wonder why he is in some pain. Yesterday they took him off of the paralytic so he was able to move his arms and legs. The first time that he moved his arms for Dad, he reached up and started rubbing my bald head. It's reassuring to me that he hasn't lost his sense of humor. We will let you know how everything went this afternoon after the surgery is completed.

Aaron

Tuesday, August 26, 2008, 8:14 p.m.

Here we are again in the surgery waiting room. We came back to the PICU after getting some supper to find many people in his room, with the drapes partially closed around his bed. Of course, we immediately thought something was wrong. The nurse then came to give us an update.

It appears that Cole's first scheduled abdominal cleansing went really well and as planned. However, afterward he was extremely uncomfortable and in a lot of pain. The nurse stated that they were having a difficult time sedating him (that didn't surprise me). The plan was to give Cole enough sedation to make him sleep through the night. That way they would be better able to control his breathing.

The first time I had seen Cole really show any sign of being afraid was prior to his going into the surgery room. It was as if he knew that he was going to be leaving the comforts of PICU, Room 15, and his Mom and Dad. I'm confident that Cole knows what is going on much more than I would previously have thought. We are waiting to be updated by the doctor.

Aaron

It is four days after the surgery and we are watching and waiting for Cole to recover so that he can get back on the chemotherapy regimen. This was the day that the doctors had originally told us that they should be able to close his abdomen, and they did try. When the surgeon made a few stitches on his abdomen, Cole immediately had trouble breathing. They quickly realized that more space was needed for the lungs to expand and they had to remove the stitches that had just been sewn. I, along with many others, assumed that after the surgery we would be well on our way back up the mountain. But Cole's lungs were worse and in a more serious condition than we realized. Normally an abdomen should be able to be closed within a week after surgery, but with Cole, it was still not closed three weeks later.

Thursday, August 28, 2008, 11:46 a.m.

Cole is back in the operating room and we are back in the waiting room. It's starting to get pretty routine waiting for the results of each operation. But it's better than nothing happening at all. The surgeons are going to try to stitch up at least some of Cole's abdomen to see if he will tolerate the pressure on his lungs. We will be praying for some better results than last time.

There are so many things that I would like to write. Contrary to much of the news we read or hear through the media, there are a lot of good (or great) people out there. It's unfortunate that we typically only hear the bad news. Why is the "bad news" considered the "best news" by the media?

Yesterday I had to make a quick trip back home to Ironwood. People asked how Cole was doing or what was the latest prognosis for him and said that they were praying for him. These are people who legitimately care about a three-year-old boy who is battling so hard against all odds.

It's been a life-changing event in so many ways for a lot of people. People whom we've never met before have offered the use of their homes here in Milwaukee, and individuals have offered to bring us home-cooked meals. When I went to the airport yesterday, some ladies had a cake and a card waiting for me. People from just about every state in the USA and from many foreign countries have in some way shown support toward us.

It doesn't matter what people say about how this world is going downhill. Don't believe it! Sure it may be more corrupt and perverted than before, but God is bigger than all that the devil has to offer. It's all of you personally that do make a difference. There are many good people out there, but you never hear the good reports about them. Have you ever stopped to think about the power of numbers and how a few people can make a huge difference? The thing is that you have to pass this goodness on to others. Bye for now.

Aaron

Friday, August 29, 2008, 10:09 a.m.

Since we have been in the hospital with Cole, it became so clear to us how we often look to the future without realizing that we are living today. When we wake up in the morning to go to see Cole, we can only think of our concern as being a "day by day" journey. The lyrics of the following song, "Day by Day," have been so comforting to me that I wanted to print them here for all of you to read. It's amazing how the Lord works. Often times I would wonder why it was so important to go to church, to fellowship, to sing hymns of praise, and read the Word. It is times like these where the songs and verses come to our minds for comfort and strength.

DAY BY DAY

Day by day and with each passing moment,
Strength I find to meet my trials here;
Trusting in my Father's wise bestowment,
I've no cause for worry or for fear.
He whose heart is kind beyond all measure,
Gives unto each day what He deems best –
Lovingly, it's part of pain and pleasure,
Mingling toil with peace and rest.

Every day, the Lord Himself is near me,
With a special mercy for each hour;
All my cares He fain would bear, and cheer me,
He whose Name is Counselor and Power;
The protection of His child and treasure,
Is a charge that on Himself He laid;
"As thy days, thy strength shall be in measure,"
This the pledge to me He made.

113

Help me then in every tribulation,
So to trust Your promises, O Lord,
That I lose not faith's sweet consolation,
Offered me within Thy holy Word.
Help me, Lord, when toil and trouble meeting,
E'er to take, as from a father's hand,
One by one, the days, the moments fleeting,
Till I reach the Promised Land.

Carolina Sandell Berg

Cole continues to be in what they call a moderate seda-
tion and has been comfortable for the most part. I think
that he is more agitated than in pain, for which I am
thankful. His recovery is still going well, and they hope
to start him on the chemotherapy regimen by the end of
next week, providing his recovery stays on course. Again,
thanks for the prayers. May we continue to flood heaven
with our requests.

Aaron

I've posted more journal entries in this chapter than the
others because we were at such a standstill with Cole. It was
a waiting game, waiting for him to recover so we could again
proceed with his chemotherapy. It was very disappointing
when the doctors didn't see the urgency that we saw for
something to happen (we didn't know what), but we knew
something needed to happen. We had watched this horrible
disease go from a tumor the size of a man's fist to filling up
a one-gallon ice cream bucket in one month. Moireen and I
knew that every day was important. Watching the days go by
one after another, with nothing being done, was devastating.
All we could do was pray.

Sunday, August 31, 2008, 9:12 p.m.

*Today is what we called a "no news is good news day."
Cole remained calm and moderately sedated throughout the
day. Cole's nurse, Sue, evidently asked him yesterday if
she should bring Dad a cake for his birthday. Cole agreed
with a nod that she should. So today, Sue surprised us
by bringing in a delicious cake. Thank you, Sue! Other
than that, there isn't a lot to report about Cole's condition.
However, I could report on Mom and how she is doing with
her pregnancy. She was able to get an appointment here
in Milwaukee this week. Everything went well, and they
look forward to seeing her in a couple of weeks. I ask for
continued prayer on behalf of Cole. Thank you and God
bless!!!*

Aaron and Moireen

Monday, September 1, 2008, 10:42 p.m.

*Hey, everybody. This is Jimmy, better know as
"Grampy" to Cole. I decided to make a surprise weekend
trip from New Hampshire for Aaron, Moireen, Karen, and
especially for Cole. I sure did surprise everyone. It was so
awesome to finally be able to see Cole and everyone else.
Even though Cole wasn't able to open his eyes, we have
been able to communicate with him by asking questions,
which he would respond to by nodding his head, "yes" or
"no." I asked Cole if he knew that Jesus loved him, and he
quickly nodded his head in the affirmative. He also seemed
to enjoy holding onto our fingers and sometimes he would
squeeze our finger as if to acknowledge our presence.*

He is still struggling with pain and labored breathing and is heavily sedated. He is fighting to hang on, so I just ask that you do not weary of praying because Cole, Aaron, and Moireen need to be lifted up more than ever.

It was so nice to be here with my wife and the others, but now it's time for me to go back home. It was also encouraging to see other visitors come to spend time with Aaron and Moireen. Some local people even brought meals this weekend. I thank everyone for the encouraging comments and for all of your prayers. God bless you all!

Grandpa Jimmy

From CaringBridge Readers

I followed your story from within a week of the time you went into the hospital. The plea of your parent's heart touched me so; you kept telling us to hug/hold our children tighter/more. I kept trying to put myself in your shoes, trying to understand what you were going through (impossible, I know, but I tried nevertheless). God used your experience to make a dramatic change in my parenting. Where I used to get annoyed or irritated by the little childish things my children would do, I now look at my five children and dear husband, and because of Cole, I smile at them more, I touch them more, I hold them tighter; they are more precious than ever before.

(State name not given)

I know you told us to send a couple of lines, so here goes, TRYING to keep it short! I gave birth to my first child in January 2008. I am such an orga-

nizational freak and need to have everything done before the light goes out at night. I would try to keep her entertained while I would run around quickly dusting or I would put her in her highchair while I scrubbed the floor. I would drag her around to Walmart, Target, the Farmer's Market, etc. I had to be here at this place or that place just to cross all the things off my list before the day was done.

I then found Cole's story, and after reading it just once, I have learned to BE THERE! Be there for her in the living room and play with her, BE THERE with her to take her on a walk, and BE THERE just to enjoy her BEING HERE. Cole has taught me something that three years of life couldn't – to slow down, enjoy, and BE THERE. Thank you Cole.

– From Wisconsin

Chapter 10

Selecting an Option

Thursday, September 4, 2008, 8:43 a.m.

At about 6:00 a.m., we received a call from the surgery person on duty. Unfortunately, she didn't have any good news. Cole's abdomen started swelling and showed signs of excessive bleeding. They arranged for him to be the first one in surgery. Please pray – he is in surgery as I write this. I do not want to give any more details until we find out some definite answers. I uploaded a couple of pictures of what the abdomen looked like this morning. The welcome page photos show how swollen it is. God bless.

Aaron

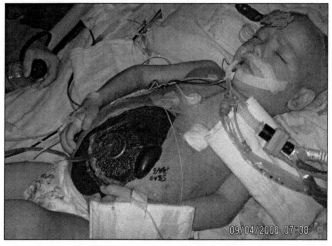

Coles swollen abdomen

Do you remember when I mentioned that this experience has been nothing short of a roller coaster ride? Here we go again, up and down, and unfortunately we are on the down side. It wasn't easy to answer the phone at the Ronald McDonald house where we were staying when we knew that it couldn't be anyone calling but the hospital. When a call is placed to the family, it normally isn't because a patient is doing well, but usually because they have some bad news. The call makes you jump out of bed, and your mind races to the worst scenario immediately.

The woman who called stated that the swelling in his abdomen had gotten continually worse. They are planning on doing an exploratory look into Cole's abdomen. Again, the news wasn't exactly what we were hoping to receive. It wasn't so much the swelling that was the problem, but it was a bigger issue than that. What they soon discovered during the surgery, was that they were now able to feel and see the tumor that was growing on his liver. During Cole's big surgery on August 22, the team of surgeons hadn't been able to see any sign of a tumor. Now thirteen days later, they could feel and see the tumor that had been growing on his liver.

When I heard the news of the tumor, I immediately had concerns about his lungs. If the tumor on his liver had grown from less than a peanut or walnut size to more than a golf ball size, what was happening to his lungs? His lungs, which were already heavily consumed with tumors at the time of his surgery, could only have been much worse now. Our minds began racing with thoughts of his lungs slowly being overtaken by tumors. It wouldn't be long before our fears started to become more and more of a reality.

At around 11:15 a.m. on that Thursday, we got official news on how everything went in surgery. The doctor told us that they really didn't have an explanation for the swelling. It was in his words: "Indescribable." They found some excess fluids but nothing near enough to cause the swelling. The doctors had all agreed that another CT scan needed to be done that afternoon. In spite of all of this, Cole never seemed to lose his sense of humor and personality. I have to share this story from the journal with you.

Thursday, September 4, 2008, 11:16 a.m.

Cole's surgery has been completed and he is awake and responding to us. The night nurse told us a story this morning that made us laugh and which helped break up the intensity of the situation. Hopefully, you will get a chuckle out of it also.

Cole had gotten a teddy bear for a gift – well, it's actually an otter. There were three or four nurses in his room this morning and they were talking to him and asking him questions. One of the nurses asked him, "Cole, do you have a bear in your bed?" Cole shook his head, "nope." "Cole, do you have a lion in your bed?" Again Cole shook his head, "nope."

They proceeded to ask him about several other animals, and as before, he answered, "No." Finally they thought they could trick him and asked if he had an otter. To their surprise he answered them with a very affirmative "YES." The funny thing is that he hardly opens his eyes to see what he has on his bed, let alone even know what an otter is. Take care.

Aaron

Hearing the otter story certainly lightened the atmosphere. However, it would have to take a lot more than just the otter story to get us through the rest of the day. It seemed as though we were back in that snowball, gaining speed once again toward the bottom. With every rotation, we were right in the middle of the snowball. With every rotation, we were getting weighed down more and more by every test and surgery and the bad news that added to the weight that was already on our backs. It didn't seem to be getting any better. It was as I said earlier – our worst nightmares were coming closer and closer to reality.

Friday, September 5, 2008, 5:25 a.m.

After viewing the results of the CT scan and talking with the surgeon, we were able to get the details of the extent of the tumor on Cole's liver. It appears that it has more than doubled in the past week and a half. Just guessing, the doctor said it is about the size of a "golf ball and a half" (his words).

The worst news is that of his lungs. The left lung is pretty much overtaken with tumors, almost to the point of not being able to function. The right lung is probably 60-75% covered. He continued to remind us of how life threatening this is. If the tumors in his lungs continue to grow, there will be no chance for Cole to be able to breathe.

Please, may we continue to storm heaven's gates? We can only trust in the fact that if God chooses to heal, there would not be anything in Cole's body that could stop Him from healing him. As the doctor told us, "In order for Cole to get better, it will only be by a miracle."

We saw how fast this disease has been overtaking his body in the last few weeks. I ask that we get as many people as possible to pray for Cole. Please spread the word to everyone that you might know to please pray.

Aaron

You know that when thousands of prayers are storming the gates of heaven you can't help but believe that God is hearing the prayers. When you feel the presence of the beautiful body of Christ (believers) lifting you up in prayer, you have been granted a blessing to take part in a wonderful event. To try to explain what it felt like is an impossible task. The only thing I can say is that at the moment the only things that kept us standing were the prayers, support, and comfort given to us by everyone. It was a part of something, that looking back, I would never give up for anything. It didn't matter what I had in life, what I had in my bank account, or what kind of house or car or any other earthly possession I owned. It simply did not matter.

It was at that time that the words in a hymn, *"This world, this world is not my home,"* took on a whole new meaning in my life. We are just travelers passing through life. We came into this world naked, and we shall also leave naked. There will not be any plaques attached to our name that will bring any glory. Nothing, absolutely nothing could compare to walking through this journey and being one of God's children. It is all about being a child of God.

We were able to experience the power of prayer in a whole new way. A few days ago we received a wooden, decorative piece that had a line of wisdom on it that said, **"When life gets too hard to stand, Kneel and Pray."** Isn't that powerful? Going through this experience, that line of wisdom is absolutely nothing but the TRUTH. Again it was the prayers from the believers that kept us going. Praise God!

When you read the next journal entry, I ask you to put yourself in our shoes. I always thought prior to this that it would be a simple decision. I know that every situation is different, but I also know that I would never have thought I would go through something like this. Never would it have to be Cole – not at only three years of age – never! Well, here we are making the decision, and I am thinking that no one should have to do this. Please think about this as if it pertains to your child. If someone had told me on the 4th of July that I was going to be in a hospital for the next two months because my innocent son was going to get cancer, I would have laughed at him or her. I didn't think things like this would happen to children, especially not my kid.

Friday, September 5, 2008, 3:32 p.m.

You know that when you're on the way to a conference room for a meeting with everybody involved in Cole's case, the news you are about to hear cannot be good. We walked into this conference room where there were seven doctors and specialists.

Never have I felt so weak, hearing only the buzzing of the halogen lights on the ceiling. There were no pictures on the walls, only the noise of a loud clock. Never would I have imagined I would be in this position regarding Cole. What we were about to hear was something that you would typically hear on the news – we just couldn't imagine going through something like this.

Immediately my thoughts went to the Terri Schiavo story that I had heard on the radio, and I thought to myself that I could just not imagine us going through the same thing. Well, here I am, twenty-four years old, my oldest child the topic of discussion, my pregnant wife next to me, and precious Chaneille back home with auntie Mar.

The grandparents were also in the room, with the exception of Jimmy, to help weigh three options. I could not help but try to picture which option God would put us in as a family, and which one would provide the best outcome. (When we talk about paths, I have already taken the path in life that we know isn't easy and is less traveled, but we know with all assurance that it has the best outcome. And that's why I chose to follow Christ.)

The hardest choice we ever had to make was which path would be best for Cole and which path God would want us to follow. The doctors went through our options and explained them in this way:

OPTION 1: In this option, we would go ahead with the chemotherapy knowing that Cole's body is not physically ready to accept the typical regimen they prescribe. We also needed to be aware that his body in its current state could very well lead to systemic organ failure and could be more susceptible to viruses as well as other typical side effects of the chemotherapy. From a medical standpoint and the doctor's perspective, this option is truly the last hope.

OPTION 2: This second option added to the confusing thoughts going through our heads. This option was to continue with how he is doing currently, taking it day by day, hoping that he will make a full recovery from the surgery and that the tumors will not continue to take over his lungs. If Cole was to recover (and be more on the healthy side), then we could start chemotherapy. The doctors most optimistic guess was that Cole would have maybe two weeks to live if the cancer continues on the path that it has been on.

OPTION 3: Remove the breathing tube that he is currently using. If we decided to go this route, he would more than likely die within minutes of the removal of the breathing tube. Once the doctors told us that, everything just started spinning. We didn't realize that Cole's lungs were in so bad a condition that without the breathing tube, he would pass away.

As you are probably able to tell, none of us wanted to be a part of this meeting. It was something that felt like a horrible dream where I was waiting for a terrible fall and where I could suddenly wake up and realize that this wasn't happening. How could we know what God would want us to do? I couldn't help but think back to Marshfield when Cole was on the breathing tube and had his first round of chemotherapy. That night, both Moireen and I prayed: "Dear Lord, please take him home. Stop the pain and let him run and play like he should. Please..." But here we were, three weeks later, still hoping and praying.

I could probably write for weeks about the special moments Cole had given all of us: When he was telling Grandpa that Jesus does love him; when we were in Marshfield and I was lying next to him and he leaned toward me, struggled to give me a hug, extended his lips to give me a kiss, and then told me that he LOVES me to the moon and back! Praise God!!! Also the times Cole just wanted us to hug or hold him, or the last special walk we had with him where he sat in my arms, and we just enjoyed every second of it. It was a blessing knowing that God truly has a plan.

But now this! How could we possibly make this decision? The only thing that seemed reasonable to us was to go ahead and give him a chance medically and accept the risks of chemotherapy. I couldn't picture myself at his funeral in a few weeks knowing that there could have been another chance for life. "Cole, we know that when your Mom or I ask you if you would like a hug and kiss, you give us a very affirmative yes. We WILL NOT let you go until we no longer have a choice. We will not give up until we can feel confident that it is your time to leave. Your Mom and I feel that God wants us to give the doctors the go ahead with the chemo – and we have the hope that the medicine will work."

We were just interrupted by the oncologist with the consent form for us to sign on behalf of the risks and the permission to go ahead with the chemotherapy. "Lord, we pray for Your blessings upon this decision; Lord God, we have no other hope but to look to You for Your healing upon Cole. We pray, Lord, for healing upon Cole's body. More so, God, we thank You for who You are and what You have already done on behalf of every one of us. We praise You, Lord. In Jesus' name we pray. Amen."

Aaron

From CaringBridge Readers

I remember when I first started reading your posts and you had written about how your perspective on a "great day" had changed. You talked about relationships and how they can develop at any random time during the day. Ever since reading those words, I have attempted to live a bit differently – as Oprah would say... a little "aha" moment! I actually wrote in your guestbook after reading that, thanking you for acknowledging and genuinely recognizing relationships in someone's life. They are so powerful!

Cole's journey has taught me that my relationships EVERY day with my three young children, my husband and all those around me are more important than I may think. I recognize that every chance I can get, I will hug my children (and I guess my husband, too :-) – sorry for the sass!) and tell them I love them. When the children choose behavior that is challenging, I try to consciously think about how I respond and how that may create a new relationship with them.

I am sorry that you had to endure this journey. It is not anything a parent should have to go through. But it must be comforting to know that so many people were affected by your story. I thank Cole and your family for helping me appreciate the relationships I am allowed to make daily.

– From Wisconsin

Cole has taught me to slow down and take one day at a time. He has taught me to hold my son a little longer each night. He has taught me to be a better mother and to not let the little things bother me. Cole, along with your family, has taught me to have a better relationship with God. I thank you from the bottom of my heart for sharing Cole with us at such a hard time. I am a better person because of your son. Cole truly was a gift from God.

(State name not given)

Chapter 11

A Time for Introspection

Saturday, September 6, 2008, 10:52 p.m. (PDT)

As another day comes to an end and as most of us have tucked our kids into bed, I came on this site hoping to find a new update from Aaron saying things are improving and Cole is doing better. Unfortunately, that is not the case. When I started this website a little over five weeks ago, I only told a few people, mostly the family. I am in complete amazement that five weeks later over 200,000 visits have been made to Cole's website. Wow, there are no words except ONLY GOD! People from all over the world have written encouraging messages and left hope written on the screen.

I have to be honest and tell you the family is growing weary. It is hard to face the unknown. Most of you don't know that we (Aaron's side of the family) lost our beloved uncle on Memorial Day and our sweet grandmother exactly one week later. It has been almost more sorrow and grief than we can handle, and now Cole.

131

There are so many names in the guestbook that I don't even know. It is just so amazing to me that so many have come to comfort Aaron and Moireen's family. You have truly blessed us! As we all get ready to go to church tomorrow, it is my prayer that we will all remember Cole in prayer and the countless others that face this awful disease! Please pass along this prayer request to all the people you know.

As for Cole, he received an epidural to help with the pain and it seems to be helping for now. He will hopefully be starting chemo tomorrow if everything goes according to plan. We pray that this dose of chemo will aggressively attack the cancer and kill it. Thank you from the bottom of our hearts for all the prayer warriors out there. Please continue to pray for Aaron and Moireen, for her parents, Jim and Karen (grandparents) and all of her extended family, for Dave and Diane (grandparents), and all of Aaron's extended family. This has been so tough! Mostly, please pray for Cole! You cannot even begin to know how much of a blessing you have been this side of heaven.

"Lord Jesus, we all come before You tonight and pray for a blessed night's rest for all of the family, especially Cole. Lord, we commit Cole to You knowing You are his Father and that You have created him perfect in Your sight. Please Lord, we beg of You that it is Your will to restore our Cole to complete health. We pray that the chemo would attack the cancer and that a miracle would be performed by You so that all would see Your mighty hand. We trust in You no matter the outcome. You are the perfect Healer and the mighty Physician. In Your precious Son's name. Amen." Bless all of you!

Cousin Julie

Sunday, September 7, 2008, 2:29 p.m.

The chemotherapy will start at 4:15 p.m. today. They thought it would be best if they waited until today, partly due to the fact that Cole has just completed another surgery. This time it was a tracheotomy, which takes the place of the breathing tube that he has had.

The timing of his surgery couldn't have been better. Being that we have been away from church for six weeks, we were able to patch in to our local church back home. The sermon was wonderful and spoke directly to my heart. Pastor Bruce mentioned how we can rest knowing that even though Cole is hooked up to these different wires and monitors he is able to rest "safe in the arms of Jesus."

We are hurting for Cole very much. Having to be in this situation, however, has been such a blessing in so many different ways. Look at all the people the Lord has spoken to through Cole and the testimonies that we have received via e-mail. All we can say is, "PRAISE GOD." It took Cole to be on his deathbed for me to stop and think about my life. What will it take for you?

I remember thinking before this whole event happened that I had my life's plans all figured out... X, Y, Z was going to happen and I was on top of my life. It was at that very moment when everything changed and I was stopped dead in my tracks, realizing Who ultimately is in control OF ALL THINGS. All I can say is, "Praise God."

As Julie mentioned in her journal entry, Cole had been given an epidural to help with his pain control. Today another central line has been put in so they will not have to use his other lines for the chemo. So as you can imagine, he is really covered in lines and IV tubes. I will let you know how things are going with his chemotherapy. Thank

*you all for the prayers, and please don't stop believing...
remember – what will it take for you? God bless.*

Aaron

Wednesday, September 10, 2008, 11:48 a.m.

*Another day of wondering... wondering if the chemo
is even touching this disease. Now it feels like it is just a
big waiting game. The last few days seem like things have
gone well, at least that's what it felt like, until one thing
happened yesterday that made me realize how serious this
is. It put a whole new perspective on living in the moment.*

*We were all relaxed sitting in Cole's room waiting out
the day, when all of a sudden a connection in his breathing
tube became disconnected. Alarms began beeping from his
ventilator, and a howl came from the end of the breathing
tube. All of his vital signs went haywire and the monitor
began sounding on his heart rate, blood pressure, and
oxygen. It was only seconds before the nurse came into the
room to reconnect the tube. You would never believe how
long a few seconds can feel when you are unsure of what's
happening.*

*That experience put a whole new perspective on living
for the moment and how serious this waiting game is for
Cole. Afterward I asked Sue, the nurse on duty, "How long
would Cole last if his breathing tube wasn't connected?"
Her response was something that I knew but didn't want to
believe. She said, "Minutes."*

*Everything really hit me at that moment. It was scary,
but at the same time a thought came to me. It was something that my Dad had told us last weekend when he was*

here. He told us how precious life is and even though it feels like Cole is really on the edge of life, he has just as much guarantee on life as you or I do. The fact is that we have no idea what lies ahead for us – no guarantee of life at any time.

Today, Cole will start his daily dose of mitotane. It has been known to produce some very undesirable side effects in the past, so please continue pleading with God on behalf of Cole. God bless.

Aaron

Friday, September 12, 2008, 6:03 p.m.

Today was an awesome day. Unfortunately, we have to rate our days by Cole's painful expression on his face, opening of the eyes, and alarms on his monitor, as opposed to what we would normally call an awesome day. An awesome day at work for me would be if everything went well on the job, the day was productive, and the sun was shining. Now an awesome day consists of having another moment with Cole.

I must confess, six weeks ago when I would think of a normal day and whether or not it was awesome, I had no thought of life or how blessed I was to have a wife at home anxiously awaiting my presence for supper and healthy kids excited to play. Instead I was arguing with Moireen about when I would get home, busy making excuses because I was late and supper would be on the table getting cold.

Wow, what a wake-up call! Now six weeks later, I'm telling the world it was an awesome day when nothing got accomplished at work. I cannot tell you if it was a sunny or cloudy day and what the temperature was. Instead we had an awesome day because Cole opened his eyes and main-tained all of his stats. Praise the Lord!

Please continue to offer up fervent prayers on Cole's behalf. Praise God. During your prayers, do not forget all who are sick and all who are battling the hurricane in the south. If you're in the south and in harm's way, please leave the area!

It reminds me of my life before Cole's cancer. If someone would have told me that my life was going to get turned upside down overnight, I would have said they were crazy. But you know what? God brought me from a point of thinking I was on top of the world to realizing that I have absolutely NO control over what the future has in store for me. When I had to give Cole over to the doctors and say, "Here he is... do what you can," do you know how helpless I felt? I'm sure many others could relate to similar feelings and stories. Anyway, I'll stop talking and leave it at that... Cole had an awesome day!

Aaron

I have no words to say other than to try to explain how mixed up my life was prior to Cole's cancer. It is with much embarrassment that I write this. God brought me out of the shell that I was in to make me realize how much more there is to life than just me. It was my mind telling me that I can do this or that – I just needed to have a plan of action.

I was always looking ahead in life the same way I planned my weekends. I recall, just a few days before bringing Cole to the ER, I came home from work and was standing in front of my work truck next to the garage door. I was looking at the "For Sale" sign in our yard, pondering my next move, thinking of us as a family at our next place, dreaming up plans for my life with my work, with our house, and with our kids. "What are they going to be like when they grow up?" I wondered. "Where are they going to live? What kind of mate will they find?" I pondered all of these life's questions in my mind so many times.

Often times it would consume me. Oh, friends, how I wish I could take back all those thoughts and just live life in the moment with Cole! We should enjoy where we are in life, enjoy what age our kids are (instead of watching them grow in our minds), and take time to enjoy life now, not tomorrow or the next day, but now. If you have a hard time taking this advice from me, then don't. Take it from the Lord who talks about these things in Matthew 6:34: *"Take therefore no thought for the morrow: for the morrow shall take thought for the things of itself. Sufficient unto the day is the evil thereof."*

He tells us not to worry, for if we worry, we do not have complete trust in Him. Unfortunately, I had to learn these lessons through the loss of someone who was more important to me than silver or gold. Please don't wait that long, I'm begging you. Don't make it take losing one of your own to realize how important this is and how blessed we are each and every day.

It all ties in to the whole concept of "Be There," because tomorrow you might not "BE HERE."

From A CaringBridge Reader

We do not know Cole or your family; what I do know is that your little boy taught me so much about life. He taught me to love more, hug more, kiss more, laugh more, and to never take anything for granted, even the littlest things. He taught me to give everything you have because you may not get another chance.

He taught me to say what you need to say because it may be the last time you get to say it. He taught me to trust in God, because He really does have a plan for us all. He taught me to live in the moment. But most importantly, Cole taught me to "BE THERE."

How much one little boy's faith has brought to my life and the lives of SO many others! We lost a baby in July. I was six months pregnant with a baby girl and we named her Rylin Audrey. We also have a four-year-old son (Kole) who has had a hard time understanding why she went to heaven.

When Cole went to heaven our Kole told us that he was okay with Rylin being in heaven now, because he knows that Cole is taking good care of her, feeding her bottle to her, giving her kisses... He also said that when she's bigger, Cole will share his chocolate milk with her and teach her how to fish. Kole is now at ease with his sister's death, knowing that your Cole is in heaven to take care of her. What a huge impact Cole's life has made on my son and our whole family.

We have come to love Cole and miss him – can't wait to meet him someday in heaven.

– From Wisconsin

Chapter 12

Cole's Final Battle

Monday, September 15, 2008, 6:23 p.m.

We just got through seeing the oncology doctor. He was unable to tell us how Cole's tumor is progressing because they have not done a CT scan in a while. They thought they would not do one until next week. We requested it be done earlier, however, so we will have to wait and see. As for Cole's current condition, he seems to be tolerating all of his chemotherapy. Every once in a while he will get very upset and pout, so you know he doesn't like it. Mitotane, for treating the cancer, is taken orally by Cole, so it could be the horrible taste that is causing him to do this. Everything else is going to have to be day by day, and time will tell. All we can do is pray.

One of the e-mails I received stated: "May Cole be healed when there will be no doubt that it was a miracle given by God." We will be praying that God heals Cole through any means He sees fit. All glory, honor, and praise will be to His name, not ours. His creation is a miracle, isn't it? Life in general is a miracle. He gives doctors the wisdom and tools to further advance medicine, but ask any doctor if things happen that are beyond their control. So far, I haven't met one that will disagree. Continue to cherish your relationships and hug your little ones.

I was reading a book today and couldn't help but share this with all of you. It talked about the only thing that really matters in life – relationships. Relationships can be built in the morning when you wake up, at noon when you have lunch, when you sit down for supper, when you celebrate your kids' personal accomplishments, or when you encourage them after their big game gets blown by a missed catch or basket. Relationships can't be built when you're too BUSY TO REALIZE what you have. God bless.

Aaron

When we talk about relationships, I can't help but think of the relationships that we have been a part of during our stays in hospitals. If any of you have ever had to stay in the hospital for an extended period of time, or had a loved one in the hospital, it's absolutely amazing what you find. You find people who genuinely care about you and your condition. You find people who can relate to how you are doing emotionally. Ultimately you find people with big hearts. It seemed like we would always find someone who would have an ear to listen, or have a voice to provide support.

I would find myself in an entirely different world at the hospital, more specifically the pediatric floor. For some reason, our hearts and thought processes change when there is a child involved. That is exactly what we find scripturally, too. Jesus had favor upon the children. It is the children we are to learn from and the children that God calls us to imitate.

A story came to mind that I would like to share with you. It's a story about Cole and how big his heart truly was. This is a story that was told by a member of our congregation after Cole had passed away. It was sometime within the past year during church when Pastor Bruce was speaking about the children, and how we need to *observe them* as they can teach us so much about how *we adults* are to be and act!

"Your family was sitting a couple of pews in front of us and I could see you clearly. You were crying, Aaron, and Cole was sitting in your lap and wiping your tears, kissing you, and smiling at you. It was so obvious that he didn't like it when you were crying and was trying to comfort you and get you to smile. Then he leaned over to kiss Moireen also! It was so precious and showed his love for both of you and the love of Jesus shining through him!"

After I heard that story my heart just stopped because I remember that particular incident. I also remember a time when Cole was in the PICU and Chaneille was in the bed with Mom and Cole. For some reason, she just started to scream and cry. It was Cole who struggled to reach up and comfort her by rubbing his hand on her cheek and telling her that it's okay. Now if that is not genuine love, I'm not sure exactly what is. It's the kind of genuine love that one could find throughout the hospital.

I remember when a little boy was brought to the PICU right next to Cole, and his parents had a sincere concern for us and Cole, even though their son was seriously injured. I could tell many stories about families we have met during our stay. I don't think I can ever thank them enough, but more so, I don't think I will ever forget them. Here was an instance where people showed compassion toward us that said more than words.

I'm probably not the only one who has said that I would pray for someone, only to soon forget about it. I could think of countless times I promised to do this and just continued in my selfish ways. Then there are the times when I would walk into a store or gas station and see a sign asking for a donation for someone who was ailing. I would simply pass by the donation jar and not even think twice.

Because of Cole, my eyes have been opened to a whole new world of hurting kids and families that need help. I will always remember the time that I was walking into the oncology area when I saw this man who immediately stopped whatever errand he was on to talk to me. I soon found out that he had a son who was battling leukemia. I believe he was diagnosed in June and it was the end of July, so he was relatively new to the chemotherapy regimen. However, the way he talked, the confidence that he had, and the support he gave me was almost more reassuring than what the doctor had told me. As I write, this family is still in the battle for the life of their son.

The word "battle" is exactly what this entire children's cancer is all about. We are fighting a war! We certainly never thought nor even heard about childhood cancer prior to July 2008. It never crossed our minds. Then it happened to Cole and us – I didn't think it was even possible. The unfortunate thing is that I'm sure that's exactly what went through the mind of my new friend whom I met in the hallway as well as the countless others who have and are dealing with this horrible disease.

Then there is the little boy, Matt, who just celebrated his twelfth birthday during our stay in Marshfield. He is and will forever be a very special part of our story. His room was next to Cole's. He was the boy who heard Cole cry and begged his mother to let him go and give Cole a hug. He was the boy, whom we found out later, was closer to Cole than anybody thought. Matt's mother sent me this story about her son, which happened the night of September 18, the night before Cole died:

Matt was sleeping when he awoke around 8:30 or 8:45 p.m. and came to get me (his mother) and demanded that I go with him to the place where we kept the fish that Cole had given us during his stay in Marshfield. Matt began to tell the fish that everything will be alright and Cole will be okay. He told the fish, "Cole even told me it was going to be okay." That continued for about 45 minutes until I insisted that he go back to bed.

Around 11:00 p.m., Matt came running into my room, yelling at me to get up. He said, "We have to go see Cole. He needs me NOW. Please Mom, you have to get up! Cole needs me!" It wasn't long before he started getting more demanding, saying, "Me go see Cole. I'm going to see Cole now!" I told him that we can't see Cole because only the family is allowed in his room, but the one thing we can do is pray. It was as if Cole came to him that night (strange, I know). But I always knew Cole was special to Matt even though the two had never even spoken to each other. They only managed to see each other a few times when meeting in the hallways or seeing the reflections of each other in the glass in the side doors of each other's rooms in the PICU.

Tuesday, September 16, 2008, 12:09 p.m.

It will be a busy day for Cole – that is if the doctors stay true to their schedule, considering the changing of his breathing tube has been delayed for three days now! Part of the reason to change the tube frequently is to help ward against bacteria. So to delay it for almost three days is beyond ridiculous to us. For those of you who have been in this situation, I'm sure you all can relate to what it's like to be at the mercy of the doctor's schedule. Sometimes as parents we think that our kid is the only one in the hospital. I guess it's only natural.

There are several things that my mind can't stop racing around and that are keeping my nerves on edge. One is the fact that Cole's abdomen continues to get bigger, especially on the side of the liver. (That is the side where the tumor still is.) I know from the past seven weeks how fast this tumor grows, and I can't help thinking that it's growing on his liver as well. Moireen and I are insisting that Cole be given another CT scan soon.

I find myself having to voice my opinion more and more to the doctors. For some reason, things are not happening, and we are getting frustrated. Sorry for venting some of these thoughts in this journal, but I tend to write what's on my mind. Clearly this is on my mind today. Don't get me wrong, because overall we greatly admire the staff. It just feels like Cole is being put on the back burner. Anyway, thanks for all of your prayers and support. We are not ready to just sit back and watch things happen. If there is anything that can be done, that's where we want to be. Sitting back while knowing that Cole has this horrible disease, is just not an easy thing to accept.

When I opened Cole's website today and clicked on the link to watch those praying for him, it was a very touching experience. First, seeing the picture of Cole standing on the bridge at Black River Harbor in Ironwood was enough to tear my heart out. (This is one of my favorite pictures.) Watching the amazing video that Lynn prepared and with everyone praying and thinking about Cole, we can't thank you enough. Your support through this is what carries us through days like today. With all of our love.

Aaron and Moireen

My thoughts and concerns throughout the last journal entry were pretty direct. I was in no way trying to criticize the doctors for their work and what had been happening. I just felt like we weren't being listened to, and the bottom line is that we weren't. I write this with my heart and I'm sure the hearts of other parents who have been in the same situation, hearts that do not intend to criticize. I write this with the hope that if any doctors would read this, they would put themselves in the shoes of the parents.

I hope that no other family would have to go through what we experienced – all I wanted was the truth of Cole's condition. I wanted the CT scan done because I knew things were happening that we were not being told. I knew how Cole's body reacted to certain medicines and how the tumor would grow in a matter of a week. I was asking for a CT scan to be done so I could mentally prepare myself for what was ahead. Instead, I got vague excuses on why a CT scan could not be done. I know all I wanted were some answers, not because I doubted the doctors or because they might be able to change the situation, but rather, because we wanted to stop wondering and start preparing for the outcome, whether it was good or bad.

Tuesday, September 16, 2008, 7:59 p.m.

The breathing tube was changed and it only took 30 seconds, thanks to the wonderful palliative care of the doctor who stepped in and turned up the heat for us. As far as the scan goes, we are having an ultrasound done tomorrow, which will give us a measurement on how the tumor in Cole's liver is progressing.

On a positive note, they take x-rays every morning at 5:00 a.m., and as far as they see, his lung tumors have not been growing like they did in the past. PRAISE THE LORD!! That's huge – if the tumors would continue to grow in his lungs, it would be very close to the end for Cole.

Thanks for all of your words of advice as far as speaking up is concerned. It sounds like many of you have been in similar situations. Goodnight – talk to you tomorrow.

Aaron

Wednesday, September 17, 2008, 3:17 p.m.

Here is a humorous story for you! Yesterday, Cole was lying in bed with a slight grimace on his face so I thought it would be nice to read him a book. He agreed with me with a head nod that he wanted me to read Thomas, so I did. Soon after I finished, we read him a book about Elly the elephant. I was hoping that it would help lift his spirits, but the grimace didn't disappear.

For those of you who have seen and visited Cole, and for the nurses that took care of him, you know that he will agree in the affirmative with the exception of a "no" if he really means it. So Mommy thought she would ask him if he wanted Daddy to read him another book. Of course, he shook his head NO, and we got a chuckle out of it. She then asked him if he wants Daddy to be quiet. He gave us the most definite YES I think I've ever seen. I couldn't help but laugh. Even Cole knows that Dad talks too much!

Cole's ultrasound was done this morning, so we are waiting for one of the specialists to come and talk to us about the results (praying for good news). Today is also the day that Robyn Niemi is coming to drop off the toys that were collected in honor of Cole. All of the toys will be donated to the children at Children's Hospital of Wisconsin. They had a lot of donations so you can expect to see some pictures online tonight or tomorrow. I will update you once we hear the results of his ultrasound.

Aaron

Wednesday, September 17, 2008, 8:21 p.m.

We talked with the oncology doctors about the results of the ultrasound. It was good news. This was not an exact comparison to the last CT scan, but the results did not show any rapid growth, nothing like what the tumor in his abdomen did three weeks ago. Praise the Lord!! It's a start. As long as the tumor is not growing, I can live with that. As far as Cole's lungs are concerned, we will have to wait and see.

Thank you to everyone that participated in the toy drive. It was a huge success. By the sounds of it, the hospital will be sorting through toys for the next few weeks. I didn't get any pictures yet but hope to soon. Take care and goodnight.

Aaron

Thursday, September 18, 2008, 10:59 a.m.

One step forward, another step back. Last night and this morning have not been the best for Cole. He seems to be having a few more bumps on the road. Whether it is a part of his chemo treatment or his lungs worsening, we don't really know. He seemed to be having a harder time breathing. So between his breathing, vomiting, and restlessness, we had a hard morning. They seem to have switched some more meds so his comfort level is a lot better. The breathing continues to take a slow bounce back up after last night. Hopefully I will be able to report better news later. Thanks.

Aaron

From time to time you hear a story where you know the Spirit of God is present in the lives of people. This is one of those stories, a story of Cole's great-grandmother, Seeri, who lives in a nursing home. She is 90 years old and battles daily with Alzheimer's disease. I hope you can imagine this picture of Seeri, who is five hours away from her great-grandchild, Cole, and probably only faintly remembers him. This is an account of the events between 9:36 and 12:00 noon on the morning of September 19.

Seeri became rather agitated and insisted that she had to go to see her family because they needed her. She was so relentless with her requests that she began wheeling herself down the hallway of the nursing home in her wheelchair. She continued to claim that her family needs her now, and that she needs to go home. This battle continued for a while with the nurse. Shortly after the nurse brought her back to her room, she went to the nurses' station to tell her co-workers that she didn't know what she was going to do with Seeri, as she is so agitated. It was then that the nursing staff informed Seeri's nurse that Cole had just passed away.

Suddenly it all made sense as to why Seeri was acting in this manner. The nurse immediately went back to Seeri's room and told her that they needed to pray, read the Bible, and talk. After the two of them did this, Seeri never again spoke about needing to go home. Ironic? Yes! Scary? NO! It's amazing how the Spirit of God works. Seeri didn't even know Cole's condition at the time (or so we thought).

From A CaringBridge Reader

Before Cole, I would find myself too busy to play with my daughter. She would ask and ask to play a game or just to play something, and I seemed to turn her down or tell her to wait. But by following Cole's story on CaringBridge, I now realize that I need to "BE THERE" for my daughter. Life gives no promises for tomorrow. Cole's story has also brought me closer to God. I thank God for every day that I have with my family, because we don't know how long anyone will "be here."

– From Michigan

Chapter 13

Safe in the Arms of Jesus

Thursday was the day in which we had all kinds of mixed emotions. We actually had been planning on taking a quick trip home to get some different clothes. We only had summer clothes with us, and here in the Midwest, it was starting to get more like winter. We originally had planned on leaving at 7:30 a.m. Before we left we wanted to see Cole. We made our way to his room only to realize that we weren't going anywhere due to the condition he was in at that time. We ended up staying at the hospital until about noon waiting for his vital statistics to stabilize and his breathing to improve. Mimi, Cole's grandma, had arrived to stay with Cole, so we headed out. Our flight was pleasurable, and the winds were certainly in our favor.

When we look back at that day, everything was so arranged by God in that all of the pieces came together in a way that we would never have been able to organize. Chaneille was actually back home with her auntie at the time, so the plan was to take her back with us when we returned. It was probably getting close to 10:30 p.m. by the time we were ready to leave the airport. I had to make the decision whether it would be a "go" or a "no go." There were strong winds from the south, and the runway was an east/west runway, which indicated that we would have a strong crosswind. We had contemplated staying the night and leaving the first thing in the morning. However, God must have had His hand in this because we went, and we were back in Cole's room about 1:00 a.m. I can't say thank you enough to God for getting us back to Cole's room before his condition started to worsen.

When we got back we were very happy to hear that Cole was awesome while we were gone. He was able to maintain all of his stats and everything was stable. It was about 2:00 a.m. that Cole's condition started to creep downhill. He was slowly losing his vital sign readings and was having a harder time breathing. We both felt that he must have been waiting for us to get back before he wanted anything to happen.

Friday, September 19, 2008, 5:31 a.m.

It was a difficult night, or should I say morning, as Cole's breathing has only gotten worse. We stayed up watching his respiration readings creep closer and closer to the limits of the ventilator. The fellow PICU doctor has ordered a CT scan today for Cole, and we will be able to get the results today. If there ever was a time for prayers for this little man, it's now.

"Lord, You know my heart is heavy-burdened. I ask, Lord, that You will give us peace and understanding to accept Your will in Cole's life. We thank You for Who You are and what You have done. So often I wonder, why me? Why our son Cole? But help us to understand. All I can do is thank You now for the wonderful and most blessed three years of my life. Help me to understand Your grace and mercy. I pray, Lord, that You will heal Cole to a complete restoration, restoration on earth or in heaven. Give us the wisdom to make the right decisions for Cole; may Your WILL be done. Lord, we praise You for Who you

are and for what You have done for us. Bless Cole and his
life. In Jesus' name I pray. AMEN."

Aaron

I will never forget that morning when we walked out of the PICU and saw the most glorious picture, which at the time didn't seem so significant. My wife had mentioned that she had seen the same thing, but neither of us talked about it until after Friday.

When you walk out of the PICU you go through a hall that has four banks of elevators, then six banks of elevators. Directly across from the elevators are two doors that lead into the surgery rooms. There are two little windows on both of the doors, probably eight inches wide by three feet high.

As I was walking by, I saw a full window of morning sunrise shining through the glass. Behind this door is a hallway that is about the length of a football field with a large, glass window on the opposite side that overlooks the city of Milwaukee. The sunrise had been creeping over the horizon providing the entire hallway with the most beautiful sunrise picture you could imagine. At the time it didn't mean much to me, but I remember it as plain as day after the fact. It was just priceless.

A few minutes later, Moireen and I were in the same area when one of the doctors, whom we respected very much, saw us in the hall. He was on his way to see Cole but stopped to talk to us. He mentioned that he had heard that Cole was not doing very well. What he meant by that wasn't that Cole only had a few hours left, but he knew that we would have to talk about his care. He had suspected that the chemotherapy wasn't going to have enough time to do its job before this monster was going to fill up Cole's lungs. He told us that he

153

had some very important questions for us to face in the next week.

I remember my thoughts immediately went to the care conference we had a week earlier where we had to make a decision on the options available to us. It was going to be a conference where many of the same questions were going to need an answer.

After we met the doctor my heart began to cry out with prayers to God. I asked God if He would please help with that decision so it wouldn't be something we would have to do. For us to make that life and death decision was much more than we wanted to do for Cole.

Now when I look back, I can see so clearly that God answered those prayers so we would not have to make that decision. He took all of our decision making out of the picture.

When the doctor entered Cole's room, he immediately noticed that we wouldn't have to be having that conversation that day after all. He told us that God had already started making the decision for us.

Friday, September 19, 2008, 9:36 a.m.

Once again, here I am at the CaringBridge website, a place to vent, a place to breathe, a place to make it through the day. I would like everyone in THE CARINGBRIDGE FAMILY to know that I can hardly type this, but everyone must know that it has been all of you that helped us get through this day by day. The doctors have said that Cole will not make it through the next few hours.

Aaron

It always seemed that when I needed a place to shed a tear, the computer would be a place where I could go and type from my heart. This was by far one of the hardest entries I had to write. I know Cole had become so close to so many and that it would not be easy for them to hear this news. So many people from different work offices told us afterward that they went through more Kleenex that day than any other. Little Cole had captured the hearts of thousands. Now here I am typing up his last few hours.

For the next hour and fifty-two minutes, we held on to Cole so tightly and kissed him so much. I was so happy that Cheneille was able to be there to say goodbye to her precious brother! The nurses soon made arrangements to get a couch in the room. Both Moireen and I were able to hold our sweet Cole in our arms until the end. It was an absolutely beautiful end for Cole. The only way we were able to tell when his last breath was drawn was by his heart rate on the monitor.

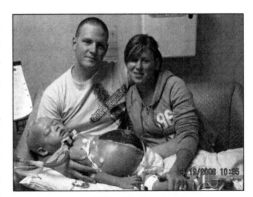

Mom and Dad's last minutes with Cole

One thing I will never ever forget for as long as I live is how on his very last breath, at exactly 11:28 a.m., Cole shed a tear from his right eye. It was a tear that was met with many tears from Mom and Dad, a tear that will never be forgotten. It was a message of love that Cole left us.

Friday, September 19, 2008, 1:36 p.m.

At eleven twenty-eight this morning,
Friday, September 19, 2008,
Cole went home to be with his Lord.
There will be no more
suffering and no more pain.

SAFE IN THE ARMS OF JESUS

Safe in the arms of Jesus,
Safe on His gentle breast,
There by His love o'ershaded,
Sweetly my soul shall rest.
Hark! 'tis the voice of angels,
Borne in a song to me,
Over the fields of glory,
Over the jasper sea...

> *Chorus:*
> *Safe in the arms of Jesus,*
> *Safe on His gentle breast,*
> *There by His love o'ershaded,*
> *Sweetly my soul shall rest.*

Safe in the arms of Jesus,
Safe from corroding care,
Safe from the world's temptations,
Sin cannot harm me there.
Free from the blight of sorrow,
Free from my doubts and fears;
Only a few more trials,
Only a few more tears!

Jesus, my heart's dear refuge,
Jesus has died for me;
Firm on the Rock of Ages,
Ever my trust shall be.
Here let me wait with patience,
Wait till the night is o'er;
Wait till I see the morning
Break on the golden shore...

– Fanny Crosby

Final Journal Entry
Tuesday, October 21, 2008, 1:30 a.m.

Here I am at 1:30 a.m. with my mind just racing. I never used to stay up this late before. Moireen would be the first to tell you that I would never stay up past 11:00 p.m., but my mind seems to be continually filled with things to talk about regarding Cole!

* * * * * * *

Dear Cole,
I'm lying here wondering how in the world I can look at a picture of you and just tell you how much I love you. Oh, Cole! I miss you so much! You're Daddy's buddy, you know that – right?
I wonder if you know how much I enjoyed chasing you around the house and how much I would love to give you another horsy-back ride. I watched Chaneille go to our room tonight on her own before she went to bed. Do you know what she grabbed? She managed to take a picture of you off the dresser, brought it to the room that you two share, and just kissed you. We miss you, buddy; we miss

your laughs, your hugs, and just the chance to play hide and seek with you... oh, how I wish I could... and maybe even read a book to you.

Do you remember how you would pretend to be a bear and chase me? Well, right now, I feel like a bear that lost its cub. I have great comfort and joy knowing that you are in heaven playing and singing songs of praise from your heart. That's not to say that I don't miss you. I wonder if I will know you by face or by presence when I go to heaven. I know your face is already a face of an angel and I would love to be able to just kiss you. But I know that you are in the presence of God, and we certainly won't be able to miss that. I wonder if I told you in person how much I love you? If you were the picture that Chaneille was holding and kissing, I think you would probably have told me to quit already. Then I wonder if you know how many people told me these cute stories of you and how much you have added to their lives.

It makes me curious why it's only when people die that we take the time out of our busy days to write a letter to someone who means so much. If you only would know, Cole, how many positive things were said about you how people said your beautiful angelic face just glows, for example. It makes me cry to think of how many times all of these nice things about you (that were true) were told to you when you were here. But then I remember how those things mean nothing because even if you would have heard them, it's not like they would actually have helped you gain your Eternal Reward. God has really shown us all a lot through your life, son... a lot about being real!

When I was lying down, some thoughts were going through my head. Why is it that in everything in life we want to show up early? You know, so we can get a good seat. It seems like everything that we do is that way: concerts, sporting events, fireworks, parades, and the list goes on...

we always want to get there early so we won't miss anything. Never do we want to be the last ones in the door because we would be looking at the backs of people for the rest of the event.

Now here is the kicker! That's true in absolutely everything I can possibly think of except for church. Why is it that those who are the last ones have to walk to the front of the church to find a seat? I am as guilty of this as anyone, but it doesn't make sense. Why do we pay extra money for the front seats, and in many cases, a lot of extra money, then when it's time for church, we can hardly give those seats away. I don't know why this is – I've never thought of this before.

Oh, Cole, I wonder what the music sounds like in heaven? What songs are you singing? Are they songs we are all familiar with or are they all new? I bet it's all beautiful... singing songs with Jesus... straight from the heart. I wonder if you miss us? Probably not, and I understand. You already made it home. Mom and I were talking the other night about how you would always tell us that you want to go home. And we were already at home! You always said that you wanted to go to your other house! I remember you would say that it would be a blue house. How I'm wondering if that blue was the sky. Oh, I bet it was!

We really miss you, Cole, but you know what? That gives me all the more reason why I want to make it to heaven. It's kind of crazy, actually. I never wanted to go to heaven as badly as I do now. Never did I want to get to heaven to see Jesus as much as I want to go there and see you now. It makes me wonder why; how... how can I do that... long to go to heaven because of my son? I think that God knew what it would take for me to realize what this whole life is all about. I loved you so much, Cole, I would have done anything for you because you were my son.

Guess what? Now I realize that God would do anything for me because I am His son. He actually loved me so much that He sent His Son to die for me!!! For ME... Cole, I don't know if I could ever have sent you to die for the world. Oh, I loved you so much. What a picture of Christ... God sending His Son to die for ME!

Cole, I do miss you to the moon and back, but all I can do is say "Praise God" for what He has shown us through your life. Jesus truly did die so that others may have life. Cole, when you died, I was able to see things more clearly. Jesus, when You died, You died so that I may have life, eternal life! Again, Cole, I cannot even begin to tell you how much Mom and I miss you! Even Chaneille. I never before saw her go back on her own to get a picture of you just so she could give you a kiss and have you back in the same room before she goes to bed. Your life was such a blessing to me and I don't know why God chose me to be your father, but I can only say, "thanks to God" for you.

Cole, we love you to the moon and back and can't wait to be able to sing songs and have eternity to look forward to, not having to worry about any cares of this world. Never will we have to worry about being separated by distance again. You truly are an angel!

Love, Dad

Chapter 14

Cole's Legacy

The life of Cole was a life that in my eyes was nothing short of a miracle. From the day he was born, there was something so different about Cole, but I could never put my finger on it. Maybe it was just the joy of a proud parent, but now I know that he truly was my "guardian angel." He taught me so much in three short years. I can only try to live up to his example of love and compassion. God blessed his life to touch the lives of thousands.

I've written this book not for my glory but that *all glory will go to God the Father.* He truly gave us the strength to endure this journey day by day. It was through His grace that we were able to be a part of a beautiful body of believers, a body that realizes that the church is not a building, but rather it's within us all. Cole was truly a vessel that God used to bring together thousands from every walk of life. For a brief moment it didn't matter what small differences there were between us; everyone was around one common bond. He was the child of whom I can say I was honored to serve as his father here on earth, and I can't wait until that day when we can meet again.

If there is one thing that I could share with you it would be this: stop and count the blessings God has given you. We can forget those blessings so quickly until God brings us to a point where we start to realize that this world is not our home. When our lives were suddenly stopped, shaken, and mixed up by Cole's cancer, it was God Who helped us withstand everything.

Pastor Bruce said it so well at Cole's funeral: "We cannot lose someone or something if we know where that person or that thing is." Today, I can't say I lost Cole because I have no doubt in my mind where I'll be able to find him. I can't wait until the day when we can meet again.

I ask you this question today: "What will it take for you?" For me, it took Cole. Please don't wait until you are in the same situation as we were before you take the time to stop and realize what really matters in life. It was a miracle how Cole could truly speak to thousands without saying a word. He was a true and humble servant of God.

In memory of Cole, a foundation has been started that is named C.O.L.E.'s Foundation – (*C.O.L.E. – Caring Openly, Loving Eternally).* This Foundation is committed to empowering families and friends to take a stand with me in loving each other – to take the commandment **"love your neighbor as yourself,"** and apply it in our lives. Cole may have lost the battle here, but in the eyes of thousands of supporters, he won the victory in receiving his eternal reward.

I want to encourage you to visit and take part in helping us in C.O.L.E.'s Foundation. One of its goals is to show the world the Love of God to those who need Him most – to stand up to this killer we call cancer. To sum up the foundation, it would be that we are simply *"everyday people helping families in crisis — EVERYDAY."*

May the legacy of Cole continue to live in the lives of thousands whom he touched in the three short years of his life.

Epilogue

Monday, October 27, 2008, 9:51 a.m.

I n one of my journal entries, I spoke about Cole asking to see me. It was about 5:00 a.m. when I went to see him in the PICU. I will never forget that moment for as long as I live. I remember walking into the PICU and Cole was wide awake. He had a smile on his face as usual. Of course, he wanted me to lay with him, so how could I pass up that opportunity? I found myself snuggling with him and he told me something that only he evidently knew. He took his hands and put them on my cheeks to pull my face towards his. He smiled with a twinkle in his eye and told me, "Daddy, I'm going to have another baby sister." Then he held up two fingers to signify that he had two sisters. He gave me a kiss and the day continued on as normal.

I guess I never really told too many people about this, or at least we never really thought about it, until this morning. I was standing behind my wife watching the birth of our newest blessing. "It's a baby girl." How could I not think about the time when Cole already told me with confidence that he was going to have another sister. "I guess you now have another girl to watch over, Cole." At 8:05 a.m. my wife gave birth to a beautiful baby girl, Whitney Mae Ruotsala (6 lb. 3 oz., 19 1/4 inches).

"Lord, we thank You for the gift of life, the blessings of having a perfect angel born to us this morning. It truly is something that only You could create and give life to such an angel. The human body is far more complex than anything we can dream up in a science lab. We are given the assurance that You are God and Your blessings are wonderful. Lord, we praise You today for Who You are and the life of our daughter. We thank You for watching over our family and having such a master plan for our lives. I ask You, dear Lord, that You would grant this girl a healthy life in this beautiful world that You have created. Help her to walk in truth and protect her. May her eyes continue to look up to You throughout her life. We thank you for Cole and the best three years that You could have given us. Now You gave us life in another way, and all I can do is say thank You."

Aaron Ruotsala

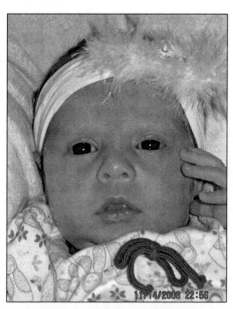

New Addition: Whitney Mae Ruotsala

C.O.L.E.'s Foundation

The creation of C.O.L.E.'s Foundation all started when Cole was going for his major surgery, an operation that was only supposed to be a few hours long, but turned out to take 18 hours.

There was an angel from Minneapolis, MN who decided to take it upon herself to start the prayer team for Cole prior to his surgery. It is ironic because not only was she an angel, but her real name is Angel as well. She began gathering troops to pray for Cole in 15-minute intervals throughout the day. Before long she had a spreadsheet filled out with names of people that represented almost every state. The prayer team was established and prayers on behalf of Cole were made throughout the day during the surgery.

The team found so much benefit for themselves that they decided to continue the team after the surgery. All of the members upheld their positions on the team throughout Cole's stay in the hospital and even a few days after his death. Angel said that the team would like my wife and me to pick another child for whom they could concentrate prayer toward since Cole had already won his battle.

Moireen and I pondered about ways in which we could incorporate more children into this prayer team, but we just couldn't make up our minds which one child needed prayers the most. They were all so important to us. It seemed that every day we were meeting new families and children at the hospital, and we built strong relationships with many of them. It was a community where you could sense true, tender-hearted people, many of whom knew exactly how we were feeling.

So the questions continued: "Do we pick Ray, Will, Matt, Brock...?" and the list could go on. We were torn, not knowing how we could pick one of these children and their families that we had grown to love. We thought of ways to get all of these children on the prayer list.

This is essentially how the groundwork for C.O.L.E.'s Foundation was laid. It was a simple matter to make a place of networking to match families to people who were open and willing to offer encouragement and hope during times of difficulty. We began assigning different children to members of the team that could "sponsor" or "adopt" a child.

We only had one simple rule: you must log on to their website and offer hope and encouragement to families and children. In only six weeks, we had over 525 children that had been "adopted," all of whom have a team member that provides encouragement through messages placed on the *CaringBridge* website.

It has been so amazing to see God working through this Foundation. In its short time in existence the Foundation has helped many people. For example: The Foundation assisted a family from Australia who had to travel to Texas for their son's medical treatment; sent Christmas cards to the children that have been "sponsored;" helped a young girl with cancer attend a concert that she desperately wanted to go to; and coordinated the giving away of tickets to a cancer patient who wanted to see an NFL football game.

We have started C.O.L.E.'s Foundation groups across the country. Essentially, each state will have their own representative, and our goal is to create a group around or near each of the major hospitals in the states. The groups are then responsible for finding different church congregations who are willing to help support the families that we have "adopted" through the Foundation. They are supporting the families by providing a meal for them, either financially (if needed) or simply preparing home-cooked meals. Again, this is another way that God has provided the Foundation with the right people to help us accomplish such tasks. In that we can be forever thankful.

We are so thankful to be able to be a part of something so great. To read some of the "thank you" letters and e-mails that we receive from the families that have either been granted a wish or simply placed on our "Adopted Family List," is enough to melt anyone's heart. I have explained it this way:

"Nothing will ever justify Cole's death or even make it feel right, except every time we make a difference in someone's life, it truly makes his death that much more bearable."

We ask for your prayers and support for this Foundation that we may be able to continue to *"Care Openly, and Love Eternally."* The Foundation's website is: *www.colesfoundation.com.*

As you are reading this, seven children in America are fighting for their lives because of cancer and won't make it through the day – seven families that need the support of all of us. Each school day, forty-six more children will be diagnosed with cancer. When our government spends 14 billion dollars a year on the space program and only 35 million dollars a year on cancer research to help prevent this killer, it's time to stop trying to put life on Mars and start helping the lives we have here now! Help join our fight! God Bless!

Aaron and Moireen Ruotsala

A New Found Love
with Cole Ruotsala

*H*ave *you ever had a connection with someone that was so incredible and so amazing that they completely changed your life in a way you never thought possible? Well that is what happened to Cole Ruotsala and me. I heard about Cole through a CaringBridge friend of mine in the summer of 2008. I saw his picture and instantly fell in love, not just any kind of love but a love that defines a life-changing event. That's when I found out Cole was diagnosed with childhood cancer. Unfortunately this sweet, little boy lost his battle on September 19 after a short eight-week fight. My life would never be the same.*

It was while driving along the Wisconsin roads (on my way to Wisconsin Dells for a family vacation) that I realized just how much this little boy and his family meant to me. It's crazy, the feelings and emotions I have toward the Ruotsala family and I haven't even met them. What does Cole mean to me? I never met sweet Cole but his inspiration is so over-whelming and just about impossible to put into words. Cole taught me never to take people for granted, that in the blink of an eye anything can happen. Cole taught me never to question God's doing and that He has a plan for all of us. Cole taught me that we are in this great big world together and that we all need to stick together and "BE THERE" for each other. Cole taught me not to count the days but to make the days count.

Cole taught me to hug a little tighter, love a little longer, and don't forget to "Be There," because tomorrow, you nor they, may not "Be Here." This is the legacy of Cole.

In October 2008, Aaron Ruotsala (Cole's daddy) created a foundation to keep Cole's legacy alive. C.O.L.E.'s Foundation (www.colesfoundation.com) is not just a foundation but more like a family. It's a family that offers prayer, support, awareness, friendship, and so much more. C.O.L.E.'s Foundation stands for "Caring Openly, Loving Eternally." It is a wonderful foundation, and I am so honored to be a part of it. Please take a minute to look at Cole's CaringBridge website and C.O.L.E.'S Foundation. Drop them a line of encouragement. You never know if you'll ever need the foundation's Prayer Team to "Be There."

* * * * * * *

Stop, Kiss and Listen
by Paula Spencer

Your child complains of stomach "owies" after an evening of pizza, playing and fishing. Did he eat too much?, you wonder. Fall down and get hurt? Is it a virus? It doesn't get better overnight. It gets worse. Appendicitis? Maybe it's something really bad, you worry on the way to the emergency room, like an appendix that's already ruptured.

You never once consider – not even after your child is transferred to a bigger hospital, not while facing the somber doctors, more of them by the hour – that your happy, hardy preschooler has a tumor. Not even as your own sucker-punched gut absorbs this news do you believe that the light of your life with the charmer grin, a little fellow who's never been really sick a day in his little life, might die.

Moireen and Aaron Ruotsala certainly never imagined a horror like that. Then they lived it.

"One day last July I was driving behind a guy I know whose dad had passed away of cancer, and I thought, 'Man, I'm fortunate I never had to deal with anything like that,'" says Aaron, who runs a concrete business with his family in Upper Michigan. Four days later, his son Cole's stomach began to hurt. "He had caught his first fish that day, a four incher that to him was a whale. He was so proud."

Cole was diagnosed with adrenocortical carcinoma, an aggressive, inexplicable cancer noted for its rarity. The odds of getting it are literally one in a million. He'd just celebrated his third birthday.

The family's summer plans of taking Cole and his younger sister, Chaneille, camping and to the lake turned into white jackets, tubes, daily stats, and the sight parents dread the most, their son writhing in pain. The tumor, the size of a man's fist on discovery, within days grew as big as a gallon-size carton. Surgeries and chemotherapy were powerless.

"Every other time Cole needed us, we'd kiss him and make it better," Aaron says. "It's the most helpless, humbling feeling you can imagine to have your son look you right in the eye and say, 'Daddy, help me!' And there's nothing you can do. Nothing but love him."

Cole died in his parents' arms on September 19, 2008. From fishing outing to a funeral in just eight nightmarish weeks.

If right about now you're itching to go hug your child, do so. That's exactly how I felt when I heard Cole's story from my cousin Mary Jo, who lives in his hometown. Looking at my kids at dinner that evening, I found myself focusing more closely on their words, not just whose elbows were on the table. I lingered one-on-one with each child at bedtime.

Sadly, this awareness tends to fade. I know well that it's all too easy to get sucked back into the morning's annoying rush of lost shoes and forgotten lunches, the barest of byes as someone slips out the door. Human nature, I suppose. (As I write this, in fact, "I'm here but not here," tapping away at my computer.)

But something about Cole's story – the tender age, the randomness, the horrible ferocity, the swiftness makes this love-one-another message especially sticky. And I mean that in the positive 21st century definition of the word.

"I remind myself daily that so long as my kids are safe and healthy everything else in my life is just 'stuff.' I hope that being mindful of these things is a small way that I can honor Cole's memory," wrote Wendy Woolford of Overland Park, Kansas, to the Ruotsalas. A perfect stranger, she happened to see a prayer request for Cole linked to a site that was originally set up to send family and friends updates about him. Now she can't forget him. Through the magic of forwarded hyperlinks, thousands of strangers sent the family messages of hope and shared how their own lives were changed.

I've noticed myself being more conscious of "de-cell-erating," as in, putting down the cell phone, turning off the screens, and really tuning in to my kids. Mary Jo says that because of Cole, she's been playing outside with her two grandsons for hours, even after she's tired. She also "adopted" two families whose children have cancer through the foundation Cole's parents set up to help some of the 10,000 other parents who go through this dumbfounding experience each year. In its first month, more than 425 people signed on to send care packages of gas cards, toys, and the thing that helped the Ruotsalas most of all – daily emotional support.

Will all of our good intentions continue? I hope so. Anyone who hears this story, at least, has an unforgettable new face on the message that, despite the crush of daily obligations, our very first obligation in life is to connect.

As Aaron says he learned in the worst way possible, "All we have are relationships. Nothing else really matters."

Incredibly, one month after burying their firstborn, Moireen gave birth to a healthy third child, daughter Whitney Mae. You bet she and Chaneille are blessed with parents who don't take one second for granted. And thanks to their big brother, the boy who lives on giving virtual hugs to thousands of kids, both sick and well, I'm logging off to find somebody to love on myself, right now.

<u>*INSPIRATION IN ACTION*</u>
About C.O.L.E.'s Foundation: *C.O.L.E. (Caring Openly, Loving Eternally), the nonprofit set up by Moireen and Aaron Ruotsala in Cole's memory, supports families whose lives are put on hold by a battle with childhood cancer. Volunteers can adopt a family and join a prayer request network. Up next: Operation Gold Rush, a nationwide fundraiser to raise awareness of pediatric cancers. (colesfoundation.com)*

This article first appeared in "Woman's Day" magazine, February 2009, as a "Momfidence" column. Reprinted with permission of the author.

Last family picture, four days before Cole's Diagnosis

Summer of 2008 – Four days before Cole's diagnosis

Cole loved his floaties for swimming

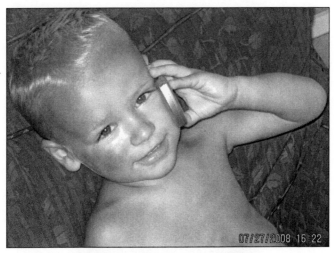

Talking with Paps (Grandpa)

**Standing on the bridge at Black River Harbor,
Ironwood, MI**

Cole with cousin Alaya -Halloween 2007

Cole, age two

Cole, age two

Additional Guestbook Letters

Dear Readers,
   The following are additional letters from Cole's CaringBridge guestbook. We are sorry that we couldn't include all of the wonderful letters that we received.
                                    – Aaron and Moireen

I'm a little shy about writing in the guestbook, but I had to let you know that I have followed Cole's site from the beginning of his diagnosis. You two have inspired me beyond words. Moireen, I'm not good at writing either. I am a single mother of two, recently divorced, and I have had some major power struggles with my faith and trust in the Lord. But since I have followed Cole's story, my faith and trust is coming back. You see, so many times Satan tried to put into my head that I was not worthy since I'm not married anymore, but God knows my heart.

   Cole has touched my life in such a powerful way. Both of my girls have blonde hair and blue eyes and I think of Cole every time I look into their beautiful eyes. I've watched the video numerous times and love hearing his little voice and sweet laugh. You two have made me love harder, hug tighter, spend more precious time with my children, and BE THERE for them when they need me.

179

I used to stress over the little things that kids do. You have taught me to be a lot more patient with my girls and enjoy them because you never know what tomorrow will bring. Not a day goes by that I don't think of and pray for the Ruotsala family.

Thank you for being an inspiration in my life, but most of all, thank you COLE for bringing me closer to the LORD AGAIN. Take care Aaron, Moireen, and Chaneille and know you are in my thoughts and constant prayers.

– From Louisiana

Cole and his family helped me to remember to be thankful for what God has given me, no matter how imperfect I think it is. God gave me this life; therefore, it IS perfect. It doesn't matter if my two-year-old has gotten up for the eighteenth time after putting him to bed, I'm thankful I have a healthy child. When 3:30 a.m. rolls around and I roll out of bed exhausted, I'm thankful that I have a rewarding job to go to. When there is constant noise in my house, I'm thankful I'm surrounded by a loving family.

The Ruotsala family has been the vessel to bring me back into a prayerful relationship with God. Before Cole, my prayer life had become one of routine; it's now amazingly personal. Before knowing the Ruotsala family, I was at a critical point in my life – very near breaking. After reading their journal from beginning to end and beginning to pray for them, God instantly lifted all of my burdens. I will always remember Cole, his family, their unfathomably difficult struggle, and their amazing example of faith and unselfish love. All my love and continued support and prayer.

– From Georgia

* * * * * * *

Cole has changed our lives. Every night we have a story at bedtime and now we have a favorite that starts... Once there was a brave little boy; he was filled with courage, compassion, and laughter...

The story ends with... When we think we're tired, or we can't finish, or something is too hard, we realize that from heaven there is Cole, along with our Lord and all the believers that have gone before, cheering us on!!!

– From Wisconsin

* * * * * * *

"I Love You." What does it take to say these simple words? I was raised in never saying those words to any of my family members. We just never did. Even though they know you love them, it is always nice to hear those words. God put those words in our vocabulary to use, so let's do it. After going through Cole's sickness, I realize I need to say those simple words to my daughters and grandkids – which I do now. Tell your loved ones you do love them before it's too late.

– From Wisconsin

* * * * * * *

Dear Aaron and Moireen,

God's Peace! I keep thinking about the memories I have of Cole and feel that now is the time to share them with you.

I vividly remember watching Cole playing under the pew in front of us at church and thinking... "I wonder if Jesus played like that as a little boy?" I don't know why I thought that and wondered about it many times. All I can think of is that we all saw Jesus shining through Cole. He was absolutely so beautiful and special!

The other time I remember (I think I shared it with you and with a lot of people), was sometime within the past year during church when Pastor Bruce was speaking about the children, how we need to watch the children, and how they can teach us so much in how we adults are to be and act! Your family was sitting a couple of rows in front of us, and I could see you clearly. You were crying, Aaron, and Cole was sitting in your lap, wiping your tears, kissing you, and smiling at you. It was so obvious that he didn't like when you were crying and was trying to comfort you and get you to smile. Then he leaned over to kiss Moireen also! It was so precious and showed his love for both of you and also the love of Jesus... again shining through him! Keeping you in my prayers.

– From Michigan

* * * * * * *

Hi Aaron and Moireen,

I have been thinking about all of you so much lately, but I am having difficulty in what I want to say. But I wanted to add my testimony to your "list" to pick from. I have been going back re-reading the e-mails we sent to each other in the beginning of September when we were planning on coming down to bring a meal. I copied part of that e-mail to be a part of my testimony. I am sure there will be testimonies a lot better than mine, but it is truly how I feel.

Here it is: "I cannot begin to tell you what a difference you have made in my life; I have always had faith in God, but Cole's story and you and your wife's faith in God has increased my faith to a point that I cannot begin to tell you. Thank you for that."

I do have more to say, but I will save that for another time.

– From Wisconsin

* * * * * * *

I thought that I'd write my little note about what Cole has done for me. I am a nurse and was sent this CaringBridge link by another nurse friend. I have a 20-month old son named Ethen. I read the journals on a Tuesday night. On Wednesday, I was to go to a nursing conference for three days. This would be the first time that I have ever left my son. I rocked Ethen to sleep and we prayed for Cole's healing that Tuesday night. On Wednesday when I left, I hugged Ethen extra hard and gave him extra kisses.

When I got home on Friday night and read the CaringBridge site and found out that Cole had passed on, I cried. I went right to Ethen and gave him an extra hug. He's too little to know what's going on, but he knows enough when Mom is sad.

Ethen reminds me a lot of Cole. I watched the videos that others had put together, and I see my son in Cole. This made me stop... and take a closer look at what is really important. Now we take our days off and lounge around in our PJ's, watching the movie Cars, reading books, or just spending quality Mommy and Ethen time.

I can never thank you enough for sharing your son's life and journey with everyone. He truly has touched many lives, more than you will ever know.

— From South Dakota

I don't remember when I found Cole's site, but there was a reason. My own 3-year-old son, Kellen, was diagnosed with leukemia on June 22, 2008. I struggled to understand and prayed to God for strength to help our family. This must have been why I was led to find precious Cole. I read his story and wept, feeling that fear for his family. Our families are so similar in so many ways. Cole's story and strength became inspiring to me. He helped me find comfort with

God. He is an angel – you could see it from the first word you read of his personality. When in this journey, you find strength in the least expected places. I'm reminded to hug a little tighter, kiss a little longer, cherish every moment, and have trust in God. There can't be anything more beautiful than being with God.

– From Missouri

* * * * * * *

Cole was a light shining in the darkness. I was so drawn to his story and I had never prayed so hard in my life. He pointed me back to Jesus. I can't wait to meet him in heaven. I will never forget your son.

> *He will gather the gems for His kingdom,*
> *All the pure ones, all the bright ones,*
> *His loved and his own.*

– From South Dakota

* * * * * * *

We have read everything on Cole right from the start. Cole taught us so much in this life that we lead. We have a 15-month old boy. We cherish more than ever all the time we have with him, whether it's bath time, feeding time, play-time, or even bedtime. No matter how bad our lives may seem right now, we leave and take nothing for granted. Cole taught us to live every minute like it's your last. Do all you want to do, when you can, and don't leave anything left undone. We've even called people that we haven't talked to in a while just to check in on them, say "hi" and that we love them. Cole has changed our lives forever. We will continue to pray for him and your family. He will never be forgotten in the everyday lives we lead.

– From Texas

* * * * * * *

You do not know me, but I have been following Cole's site for some time now. I signed your guestbook a few times and was so struck when I first saw Cole's picture because he reminds me so much of my 2-year-old son. My son has an incurable neurological disorder called Sturge-Weber Syndrome, and we also have a CaringBridge page for him. Anyway, I wanted to congratulate you on the job you are doing to raise awareness of childhood cancer. Like you, my husband and I are on a desperate mission to raise awareness for our son's very rare illness. It is an uphill battle to "spread the word" and make people aware. But we believe two things. One, knowledge is power, and two, if you reach out, amazing things can happen. You and your family are a true inspiration, and there is not one day that goes by that I don't think about little Cole.

– From Massachusetts

* * * * * * *

My children have a more loving and grateful mother thanks to Cole. Everyday I praise God for the gift of His messenger – sweet Cole. This boy made me stop counting my money and start counting my blessings.

– From Texas

* * * * * * *

Hi Aaron – I wanted to start by saying thanks for visiting my son Sam's CaringBridge site. One thing that has recently hit me is how many CB sites there are out there for kids, many of which I came across in your guestbook and took time to visit. It can really be depressing to think about how many parents are going through the same pain and heartache that you and Moireen are. I found myself wondering how many of them do not believe in God and how much harder it must be for those that don't.

You asked in one of your entries for people to send you ideas for things to do for Cole and for statements of how he changed your lives. I can tell you that I love the idea for the foundation and for the book. I also like the idea of making some sort of magnets for the refrigerator or something to hang on the bathroom mirror with a picture of Cole for people to see every morning that reminds them of how not to take life or their precious children for granted. I personally have two of Cole's pictures hanging on my refrigerator and it has made such a difference. One look when my kids are driving me crazy and it immediately softens my heart and makes me respond to them in a much more loving and constructive way.

As far as how Cole and your family have changed my life... well, I've been thinking of how to put that into words for some time now. Then I read the entries in the guestbook and realized that pretty much everything everyone says reflects exactly how I feel as well, so I don't know if I can add much more to that. I suppose the best I can say is that this whole experience has touched me profoundly in a way that nothing else in my life ever has. I've tended to be a fairly pessimistic person in my life, and getting our son's diagnosis when he was 2 1/2 years old didn't help much. But even after going to church for 37 years and looking for that one thing that would turn things around for me and help me to appreciate the things I have, nothing has ever worked that well... until Cole.

I've always adored my three boys, of course, but the stresses of life tend to get us down. I know that I haven't been as understanding and patient of a mother as I could have been. It's always easier to lose patience and yell than to just sit down and take the time to try to understand why they are being the way that they are. Having Cole's picture on my fridge has significantly helped with that. For the first time in my life, I feel such deep gratitude for all of the things in my life. I have so much more patience not only for my kids, but for others as well. I wake up in the morning and I notice the warm, fall air, and the beauty of the fall leaves, and I am so thankful to be able to share that with my family. It sometimes freaks me out how deeply this all has affected me.

I didn't find Cole's website until four days before he died, but in that week, I read the site from beginning to end, spent hours crying and praying, and sitting by my boys' bedsides watching them sleep and praying that you'd be able to do that with your son again. When that didn't happen, I was truly heartbroken. I cried all day at work that day, and my co-workers probably thought something was seriously wrong with me, but nobody ever asked. On the way home, I was talking on the phone to my husband and we had the exact conversation that you published a few days ago. I was sad and angry and telling him that of all the people that had visited Cole's website, there had to be some who had doubts about God. There have been times when I have had doubts, and this would have been the perfect time for Him to give that miracle – to put to rest all of the doubts of those who were following Cole's story.

How could He have given up that opportunity to reach that many people all at one time? My husband's answer was that the miracle was just how this whole thing brought everyone together in such an amazing way, and that in the end, Cole was really the one who got the miracle and was in eternal peace.

I've shared his website with so many people, and I've encountered so many other people just in everyday life who are being nasty or ungrateful or unkind to others and wished I could go up to them and tell them about the website as well. This experience just puts everything in a whole new perspective, and it frustrates me now to see people who are so caught up in the small, insignificant things of life.

Sorry to be writing a book here, but I've had a lot on my heart for a while now and just wanted to share. I guess that I really want to say is THANK YOU for sharing your son with me, for being so honest about your experience and your feelings, and for the incredible strength and faith that you have shown to everyone through all of this. THANK YOU for changing my life for the better and for making me a better Mom and a better person. It's so obvious what God's plan was for Cole, but I hope you realize that you were the voice of that plan, and without you, his death would have been just another sad story that only a few people heard about. There are many people out there who have endured what you have... some choose to be angry and bitter and others use the experience to do amazing things. You have such an opportunity for ministry, a lot of which you have done already, but it can go so much deeper. I suspect from your writing that you have heard that calling. I hope that it has made things a bit easier for you to able to express your feelings through Cole's website and that you have many people writing and praying for your family's healing. l know it will be hard for quite some time, especially with the new baby coming and the holidays right around the corner, but I hope those things will also give you some renewed peace and joy. I can only imagine how much you must cry, as I do almost daily, and I've never even met Cole or your family.

It's just strange that I feel such a connection to you all. As I've read about how sweet and angelic Cole was, I found myself thinking that the only thing more perfect in this story would have been if his name was Gabriel (the angel). But then I couldn't help but chuckle because that is the name of my youngest son. He was due on Christmas Eve and was born on December 27 (exactly six months after Cole), so he got the Christmas name. The reason it's kind of funny is that he is just a spitfire... he's the most busy, stubborn, and sometimes obstinate child I have ever seen... hardly living up to the angelic name at times. But in all fairness, he does have times of incredible sweetness and innocence, so I know he has potential.

I hope you and Moireen and Chaneille sleep well tonight with dreams of your own precious angel to touch your heart and give you peace. I'll be checking in on the website frequently to keep up with your family and how you are doing. I don't know when your baby is due, but it sounds like it may be soon, so I hope you'll share that news with us. Peace, blessings, and gratitude to you all.

– From Kansas

* * * * * * *

I wanted to let you know how Cole and your family has touched my life. Somewhere along the way I lost what was truly important in my life. Cole showed me that I am the luckiest person in the world to have two wonderful little boys and husband in my life. He helped me to remember that everyday is a blessing and a gift given by God. I now make sure to enjoy every moment with them. I will dance with them, sing with them, be silly and love them with all that I have and all that I am.

I will not sweat the small stuff because it's the small things like the "I love you" and the hugs and kisses that are the greatest things. Thank you Cole. You will always be a beautiful soul shining down on all of us. I will never forget.

– From Wisconsin

* * * * * * *

I would love to tell you how Cole changed my life. For me, it was not to just "Be There." I AM there with four kids. I spend my days sitting on the floor playing My Little Pony, finger painting, and playing chase around the kitchen. After school it's every sports game, every class party, event, and school event. There is so much running around trying to "be there" that sometimes I forget to just "BE." I couldn't agree more with the girl that posted... "don't count the days... make the days count." That is what we are now doing. My kids don't need "Supermom," they just need Mom. We don't need to have schedules so hectic that I need two pots of coffee to get through the day. I am no longer available to just "be there," I am available to "be with" – to "be together." We are cutting back our extra curricular activities and spending more time doing absolutely nothing... TOGETHER.

My biggest fear has been death – mine, my childrens', my husband's, parents'... anyone in my family. I am an avid "please bless my family and me with long, HEALTHY lives" prayer. I always have been. If I am being totally honest, I am so afraid of things like sickness and death that I could never be one of the people that visit tons of CaringBridge pages.

Then in July I got an email from a MOPS group about Cole. Everything changed. I don't know what made me go to CaringBridge. Maybe it was just that I couldn't understand how another mother's child simply had a bad stomachache and was diagnosed with incurable cancer. How does that happen? I have no idea how I even got the guts to follow the link, but I did. And Cole changed me. He had me that first day with that first photo. I followed both Cole and your journey daily. There were many nights that I couldn't sleep because all that I could do was lie in the dark and pray and beg God to help Cole. During my daughter's nap times, I would read the guestbook entries of love, faith, and commitment to life... to miracles... to God. There were so many believers who knew that God had a plan.

I believe in God. I believe in the power of prayer. I believe that if you are good here on earth that you get to go to heaven. I believe that God forgives sins, but even though I knew these things, it just didn't really ease my fear of death... until Cole... until your family showed me. I realized how everyone truly understood that heaven is the goal, not an end result. Heaven is really a place. Heaven is a place where there is a little blond-haired boy named Cole, playing in sunshine flooded fields of flowers. There is no sickness there. It's always summertime. There is no heartache, there is only love, and the love that Cole took there is from you and from me... from all of us. We are with him just as he is with us. Love is eternal.

I am not afraid of death anymore. I understand I will always continue to pray for my family to live long, healthy, and happy lives... because that is love. When it is our "time" to go, we will carry the love with us to a higher place.

May God bless you and your family. Thank you for all that you have given to us. Cole may have been the hand of God that brought us all together... but you hold the pen. What you do with it counts.

– From South Dakota

* * * * * * *

During the time you were struggling with Cole's illness, I was struggling with my 16-year-old daughter's rebellion and quest for more independence. Often, I would end the day in tears, thinking I had failed God and was losing my daughter. It was so painful that I decided I would let her go – I didn't care anymore what she did or how she acted towards me. I gave up.

I saw through your journal how hard you were fighting for Cole and how much he meant to you and Moireen. You weren't giving up when you faced even greater obstacles and emotional pain than I could ever imagine. So, I fell before the Lord time and time again and pleaded for my daughter and my relationship with her. I apologized to her for the things I had said to her, the way I had acted, and asked for her forgiveness. There was no response from her. Last week, she came home from Youth Group and apologized and asked my forgiveness for what she had done.

Our relationship has been restored and I have Cole and your family to thank for that – without you and your examples to me, my relationship with my daughter would still be estranged and I would be miserable. I have thanked God again and again for your example. While I am writing this through tears, this is the first I've been able to go back to the CaringBridge website. I felt I needed to let you know my life has changed because of a little boy and his family that I have never met on this earth, but whom I will be spending eternity with praising our almighty God and His precious Son, Jesus Christ.

If you would like to see a picture of my family (minus my husband), we are in the third group of Cole's prayer warriors. Sarah (my 16-year-old) is the one in the sunglasses in the middle of the three kids.

In Him who sustains!!

– From Minnesota

* * * * * * *

I found this on a friend's care page for her son and thought of you right away!!! Enjoy...

Once upon a special day
In heaven up above,
The tiniest souls sat at God's feet,
Surrounded by His love.

The time was coming, very soon...
God said, "Do not be scared.
Your family awaits your arrival,
Now let us get prepared."

And so, God looked upon these souls
In mute consideration,
He knew the life each one would live,
He weighed each situation.

The souls chatted amongst themselves
And wondered who they'd be -
They knew the day grew closer... soon,
They'd meet their family.

"How would you like to change the world?"
God asked each soul in fun;
"The chance to make a difference
Is held by only one."

"I'm going to make the world laugh,"
One soul said with a smile;
"For laughter heals a broken heart,
And helps us through each trial."

"Then take with you the brightest smile...
And share your laughter well,"
The soul thanked God immensely,
And down to earth he fell.

"And I'll remind the world to sing,"
A sweet little soul told the Lord;
"I have the gift of a beautiful voice,
I can hit every note, every chord."

"You'll have the gift of music, then,
A voice, lovely and strong;
Share your gift with others,
And let them hear your song."

"I will show compassion..."
The next little soul raised his hand.
"Some people only need a friend,
Someone to understand."

"Compassion is a good thing."
God said with much delight.
"To you I will give mercy,
You'll perceive wrong from right."

And so each soul... shared every thought -
Their plans, their hopes, their dreams;
As God explained that life, it is
Much harder than it seems.

And as each soul began to leave
In a scurry of laughter and fun,
Heaven became quiet -
Left, was only one.

"Come sit with Me, my little child,"
God said with just a sigh.
"Do you know how many you will touch,
In a world left wondering why?"

"From the moment that your life begins,
You will know of strife;
But you'll teach those who know you
To cherish the small things in life."

"And some may only know you
Through a simple photograph;
They'll never hold you in their arms,
Or memorize your laugh."

"Some may only know you
Through the words they read each day; But you'll do
   something wonderful -
You'll make them stop... to pray."

The tiniest soul raised her head up
To touch God's firm, strong hand;
"Father, I am ready for
The life that you have planned."

"And I will do the best I can,
Without a word or deed;
For You, Lord, are the planter,
And I will be your seed."

She could already hear many praying,
And although they had not seen her face;
They were praying for her safe arrival,
They were asking for mercy and grace.

"What talent do I leave with, Lord?
What gift do you impart?"
"All that you will need," God said,
"I've placed within your heart."

And so God kissed this tiny child,
Knowing all that she would be;
And whispered as He watched her go...
You'll teach them... to see Me.

– By Stephanie Husted

– From Minnesota

I just wanted to say thank you so much for sharing your precious child with us. He absolutely changed my life. Being a 21-year-old woman, I don't always put things into perspective... and Cole did that for me. I found Cole's website by "accident," but after reading about him, falling in love with him, and following his journey..., I know it was by no means an accident. Every day I found myself running to my computer to read about his status, check new pictures, and I often found myself crying.

I wondered how someone I had never met, who was 18 years younger than I, and lived 300+ miles away could change my life... but Cole did just that. He opened my eyes to a new kind of love, the love of a mother and father to their child and, of course, a child to his mother and father, the love of brothers and sisters, and the love of complete strangers... joining together in love. Cole brought many laughs, tears, and questions into my life. HIS courage taught me to be courageous, to stand for what is right and what I believe in. He taught me to love wholeheartedly and without reservation. He taught me patience, loyalty, and the power of believing.

I watched the videos of little Cole... and I cried through every word. When he spoke on the phone and would repeat "huh?" over and over, I laughed and I cried, and I longed to meet him. I wanted to know this little Hero. I wanted him to know that I cared for him and thought of him often, and prayed for him several times throughout the day. But as silly as it sounds, I know that Cole knows. Not only that I loved him and cared about him and thought about him... but that thousands of others did too. I am sure that he felt the love and those prayers.

It makes me so happy to know that he is in heaven. He is dancing, laughing, and sitting on our Heavenly Father's lap. He is singing, playing, and loving your family SO MUCH. Cole was a precious, precious child... and I hope you feel so honored and lucky to be his parents. God must have thought the world of you both to put an earthly angel in your arms.

One more thing before I close. I saw a sign the other day and it made me think of Cole. It said, "If love could save you, you would live forever." Love did save Cole. The love of Our God saved him... took him home... free of hurt and pain... and YOUR love saved him here on earth... you comforted him, loved him, and made him into the ideal child. I will never forget Cole. Thank you, thank you, thank you... that's all I have left to say.

– From Indiana

* * * * * * *

I have been reading your CaringBridge page for Cole since I learned of your family through a friend's grandson's CB page. I did not learn of Cole until the day he went Home, but his story and the story of you and your wife have touched my heart in so many ways. The first time that I visited Cole's page and read his story, I cried. It surprised me how deeply it affected me to see your pictures, read your words, and then absorb the reality of what was happening in your world. The frustration that this kind of thing happens to our sweet, innocent children was overwhelming. But your words and the evidence of your faith were so compelling. There were so many conflicting feelings, and Cole weighed on my mind for days. I signed your guestbook and found myself getting the e-mail updates every time you wrote in your journal. For several days I read them daily, but it was so overwhelming that I unsubscribed. I didn't want to feel that pain for you every day. Even still, Cole and you and your family weighed on my mind daily. Today I found myself drawn back to you and I searched and found Cole's page again. I wanted to check in on you and see how you were doing. I was pleased to see the journal entries and the commitment you are making to carry Cole's legacy forward. You are a special young couple in so many ways.

I am sending you this to share how Cole's story changed me. When I read Cole's story, I was sitting at my desk working, a spot I find that I spend most of my waking hours. I own my own business and it runs me more often that I run it – or so it seems. That particular day I was so stressed and so overwhelmed with life in general. When I read Cole's story, I cried and cried and cried. There were so many thoughts, but there was one that stands out. Here I sit, worrying about my business, worrying about money, worrying about what step to take next, and somewhere in this big world sits a young couple mourning the loss of this special child. It puts so many things into perspective for me. I read your words in one of your entries about how this had changed for you – how you would call home and tell your wife you would be home soon, but that you spent more time at work and thinking of work than you had realized. I realized that I was in the same boat. My children are grown and gone now, but I still have allowed time to drive down a road that turned me into a robot, a robot that thinks of little else but work and existing. I realized that there is so much more that is important – so much more important.

A day will come when I go Home too, and what will I leave behind me when I go? An empty chair at my desk? I made a conscious decision that day to not let work and bills drive my decisions quite so much. I made a decision that at the end of the work day, I would go home and be with my husband instead of working into the night and falling into the bed exhausted. I made a conscious decision to stop and take a call from my child even if I was in the middle of a project. I made a conscious decision to spend the money to buy a flight to go see my child, even if I was afraid it meant the light bill may not get paid this month. I made a conscious decision to trust in HIM, that if I did my best in all areas of my life, HE would provide what I needed to live. I guess in short, the day I read Cole's story, I made the decision to give up control of my life to our Lord and stop trying to control the path I am on. The fact is that we have very little control. No matter how much we may fool ourselves into believing otherwise, HE is in control and HE will lead us through whatever HE brings us to. This is the lesson Cole taught me that day.

Since that day, my stress level has leveled out and my overall sense of well-being has increased. I still have a journey ahead of me to truly live the convictions that I have shared with you, but it was you and your family that brought me here, and I wanted you to know. More importantly, I wanted to thank you. Thank you for sharing your pain, your joy, your story, and most of all, thank you for sharing your Cole.

You may share any part of this you wish, but I prefer you keep my name private. I also want you to know that it is not only Cole that has touched so many, but you and your faith, and your strength, and your willingness to be open, and human, and loving, and caring, and weak, and strong, and certain, and uncertain, and just you. You are a powerful young man, and I can see that as you walk forward you will do well for yourself, for your family, and for those you are able to touch. I believe that God has gifted you in many ways. I pray that you will find the guidance you need in your heart to move forward and find the peace and happiness that you deserve.

My prayers will be with you and your family always.

– From Georgia

* * * * * * *

I have been following your story on CaringBridge since I heard about Cole's tumor in August. For some technical reason, I wasn't able to send a message to the guestbook. I wanted to let you and Moireen know that I and my family and friends here in Finland have been praying for you and your son Cole.

I saw the video of the funeral, and it was awesome. I'm so glad that you wanted to show it for us who have been following your family and little Cole on CaringBridge! I'm glad that Cole doesn't have any more pains – he is free from all of these worldly things. Thanks to God that Cole is at home in heaven. I'll continue praying for you and your family, that God would strengthen you in your sorrow!

I would like to send this song to you. Although it is in Finnish, it tells us about the love of God for us and what he has promised for his children in heaven above.

In English:
I Have Heard of That City of Wonder

Olen kuullut, on kaupunki tuolla
Yllä maan, päällä pilvien usvain
Luona välkkyväin taivasten rantain
Siellä kerran, ah, olla mä saan
Hallelluja, mun lauluni raikuu
Halleluja, mä kaupunkiin kuljen
Vaikka jalkani uupuen vaipuu
Joka askel mun kotiin päin vie

Olen kuullut, on maa ilman vaivaa,
Ilman kyyneltä, taistoa, kuolta
Kipu, sairaus, tuskaa ei tuota
Siellä kerran, ah, olla mä saan
Halleluja, siel' riemuita voimme
Halleluja, jo epäilys haipui
Enää koskaan en horjuen kulje
Olen saapunut Jumalan luo

Olen kuullut, on valkoinen puku
Ja on hohtavat kultaiset kruunut
Sekä autuas taivainen suku
Siellä kerran, ah, olla mä saan
Halleluja, nyt henkeni kiittää
Kun jo kuulla voin taivaisen laulun
Side katkee mi' maahan mut liittää
Tiedän, siellä jo pian olla saan

Halleluja, nyt henkeni kiittää
Kun jo kuulla voin taivaisen laulun
Side katkee mi' maahan mut liittää
Tiedän, siellä jo pian olla saan

– From Finland

You don't know me or my family, but we have, however, gotten to know you (or so it feels like) so well through all of the wonderful things that friends have told us about you and your family. I have followed Cole's CaringBridge site since I first heard about all of this. And as soon as you mentioned the To the Moon and Back Foundation, I felt like I had to tell you this story. Since I'm not sure how many of the CaringBridge entries you both get a chance to read, I wanted to post this story to both the CB and by e-mail, hoping that you would get a chance to read it. (The following is what I posted on CB on October 3.)

Out of suggestions that you have been given, I personally LOVE the idea of the "To the Moon and Back" Foundation! There is actually a personal story behind the title that I would like to share with you. My 6-year-old son, Trevor, has been saying "I love you to the Moon and Back" to me nearly every day since he first started talking. And every night before bed, he will say, "I love you to the Sun and Back." Well, the other night after I read his book to him, he said, "Mommy, I love you to the Sun and Back... and Cole loves his Mommy and Daddy from Heaven and Back." My heart dropped when he said this. Every time we say this to each other, I now seem to cherish it even more since it not only reminds me of the loving boy, Cole, but it also reminds me to cherish every single word that my son says. (Thank You COLE!!!)

I just wanted to share this story with you because it is just absolutely amazing to me how many lives Cole has touched... including ours. God bless both of you and your families.

– From Michigan

* * * * * * *

I have been struggling with writing this e-mail – like Moireen, I'm not a writer. I just came across Cole's CaringBridge site last Friday (October 3) and could not stop until I had read all of your journal entries. I found myself thinking and weeping for Cole and your family all the time. I can't imagine how you and Moireen were able to get through Cole's time in the hospital. We all ask why Cole had to leave his family being so young, even though we will never get the answer. I admire you being able to stay so connected to your faith. I'm not sure I could be that strong.

No child should ever have to endure the pain that Cole did, and no parent should ever have to feel so helpless. We have so little control, and all we can do is be with and love our children. The precious stories of Cole smiling and trying to comfort you as he was fighting this horrible disease shows he may have been afflicted with a rare cancer, but he was clearly a "one in a million" little angel. Cole has taught me I can't hug my kids tight enough or tell them often enough how much I love them. I hope writing the book will help you with your heartbreak. I look forward to reading it. Your strength and faith inspire me to be a better person.

– From Illinois

* * * * * * *

I have never met Cole or his family, but somehow I believe through the grace of God I was directed to his CaringBridge website. I've looked at other CB websites in the past, but something kept drawing me back to Cole's site. Was it Cole's infectious smile and those big blue eyes? Or maybe it was the great love that Cole expressed for his little sister, Chaneille, and his Mom and Dad, even when he was feeling at his worst.

The morning of September 19, 2008, my heart sank. I was praying for a miracle like so many others, yet relieved that Cole was no longer in pain and that his suffering had ended. From the moment I read about Cole and his journey, I know my life had changed for the better. This sweet 3-year-old little boy has taught me what really matters most in life – that no matter how tired I am at the end of the day, to always make time to color a picture or play with my children. And last but not least, I never take life for granted. Thank you, Cole. I will never forget you. Thank you, Aaron and Moireen, for sharing your son Cole's legacy.

– From Minnesota

* * * * * * *

I began following Cole's site at the beginning of September when a friend told me to check it out. I have a 19-month-old son who has the same white hair as Cole. He was even a cowboy for Halloween last year! My husband and I are 25 and 24 years old. I look at Cole's picture and see my son. I am so sorry for your loss, but I wanted you to know what Cole has taught me.

Cole has taught me to slow down and take life one day at a time. He has taught me to hold my son a little longer each night. He has taught me to be a better mother and to not let the little things bother me. Cole, along with your family, has taught me to have a better relationship with God. I thank you from the bottom of my heart for sharing Cole with us at such a hard time. I am a better person because of your son. Cole truly was a gift from God. Thank you.

– From Wisconsin

* * * * * * *

I know that we don't know each other, but like so many others, I have been so touched by your story from the first day you posted an update and pictures of Cole on the CaringBridge website. You two have been on my mind so much lately, and I have cried many tears for your loss. I have a 2-year-old son who is a little blue-eyed blonde. So many pictures of Cole remind me of my little guy. I understand the love a parent has for their child. It is so strong and big that it's actually indescribable, isn't it? I know that I cannot understand what you two are facing and the pain that you are feeling. I have tried to think of words to offer... but I know there are no words to take away the pain. But I did want to share something with you that really touched me and instantly made me think of you.

This past Saturday I had been thinking about you and praying for you when I sat down on our couch to feed our 8-

week-old baby. I turned on our TV to help pass the time. For some reason all of our stations were fuzzy except for TBN. There was a man being interviewed by the name of Robert Rogers. He started to share his testimony and I was blown away by the strength and comfort God has given him.

A few years ago he lost his wife and his four beautiful children in a tragic accident. His story is absolutely amazing. I cried there on my couch as I watched a slide show of pictures and home videos of him with his wife and children... so many precious memories. He wrote a song to his wife and children that was so beautiful, but I haven't had any luck in finding it online. I was hoping to send the words to you. I really think you would have been blessed by this man's story.

I have never lost a child, but this man lost his entire family... and is able to praise God, and He is using him in a huge way! He said that he could be bitter because of what he's been through, but God is making him better instead. He said he refuses to be a victim but a victor through Christ! Wow!

I just wanted to let you know his story in hopes that it might be encouraging to you. He has a website at www.intothedeep.org. There are different links on the site where he shares his story and shows how God has been so faithful. God is using his family's legacy to touch thousands, just like Cole! Now I know why all the other stations were fuzzy... I guess I needed to hear that testimony!

Aaron and Moireen, I will continue to pray for you, for your precious little girl, and the new one on the way. Every day my heart just aches when I try to imagine what you are going through. Just tonight when I read about Moireen crying in the bathroom, it absolutely broke my heart again, and I went and cried in our bathroom.

I hope and pray that God gives you the strength to BE THERE for each other so you can weep on each other's shoulders... and how I pray He gives you the comfort and even joy of knowing precious Cole is finally home with His Creator, and you will see him again some day! Sorry that this is getting so long. God bless and keep your family. With lots of love and prayers.

– From Michigan

* * * * * * *

We, like so many others, do not know each other, but I feel like I do to an extent. This summer on July 6, my husband was in an ATV accident and suffered a spinal cord injury and is unable to walk. He needs assistance with many of the daily things we all take for granted. Through his CB site, I found Cole's site, and my husband, my children, and I were just drawn to it. The strength that you have shown has literally gotten us through this difficult time in our life. Cole is still talked about everyday in our home and we continue to pray for you. There have been so many days that my husband and I have questioned why things happen in life, and why us? Cole has held us up and guided us through all the challenging days we have had and will continue to have in life as we learn all the things that have changed for us. Cole and your family have been there for us and changed our lives and made each day better... and I thank you for your strength and for sharing your beautiful son with all of us. God Bless.

– From Minnesota

* * * * * * *

Dear Aaron and Moireen,
You guys are such an encouragement to me because of your strong faith and amazing love for each other and God!! My family and I are still keeping you in our prayers! I have read that you wanted memories that others have of Cole, so I thought that I would tell you of some of mine.

I don't think anyone could ever describe what a blessing he was. How do I describe such a precious boy? I took him for granted. Never in my wildest dreams did I think that my precious Cole would get such an awful disease and pass away before my eyes. Never did I think that soon I would have to say good-bye for the last time. I loved him soooo much and I still do! Only a babysitter knows how attached you can get to kids. They become a HUGE part of your life, a part that will never leave nor can be taken out. When I think that I will never see his gorgeous blue eyes again or hear his tinkling laughter, my heart nearly breaks. I will never again see that on this earth. In heaven, where Cole is a perfect baby with no ailments or pain... then, only then, will I see those precious things.

Looking back, I wish that the last weekend I had with him that I would have held him longer, hugged him tighter, and kissed his precious cheeks until he no longer liked it. That weekend, I had to give him a timeout for biting Aiden. He sat perfectly silent as his cousins played outside. I sat on the other couch and glanced through a book.

I had set the time for about five minutes, and when the alarm rang, he could be done. He was very good and I wish you could have seen his face light up when he could leave. Wishing isn't going to change anything, but I wish that I could have five minutes with him again, and I would never let go of him. I will miss him as long as I am alive and will never forget him!

Another cute memory (one that I shared with Moireen a while ago), was where the kids were running around Angela and Jason's island-like area. Cole's pants kept slipping down, and the other kids were telling me, "Cole took his pants off!" So I told him, "Cole, don't take your pants off." He looked at me innocently and kept on running while holding the waistline so as to keep his pants up. It was soooo cute!! Afterwards, I tried to make him a belt out of a garbage bag.

He didn't have a belt, and as Abby pointed out later, there were some little straps that were in the waistline. He was confused but cooperated as I talked to him about what I was doing. Then Abby showed me the straps and we fixed it so he could run without his pants dropping. He was such an angel here, and in heaven too, I'm sure.

Cole has blessed my life and made me realize that those you love are not always around. Cherish them and make sure that they know that you love them. I will always make sure to tell those people more often. I loved Cole and always will. I cherish the moments that I remember and have of him. He will always be my precious Cole. Thank you for allowing me to be a part of his beautiful life.

– From Michigan

* * * * * * *

Thank you for sharing your blessing (Cole).

Thank you for showing and sharing the amazing faith God has given you. I have followed your journey with Cole ever since I got that first text message that said your little boy was sick. I have not signed your guestbook or written to you yet, but had many thoughts and been VERY touched by it all.

Lately I had been wondering why I, like so many others I'm sure, have such an urge to visit your page many times to see how things are going. While considering this, I was searching my Bible and was led to Galatians 6:2, where it says, "Bear ye one another's burdens, and so fulfill the law of Christ." So after reading this I believe we come to you, remembering you, and praying for you, hoping to help bear your pain of loss and to rejoice in Cole's victory of eternal life, free from all suffering and pain. All glory, thanks, praise, and honor be to God for the blessing of Cole's life and the wonderful work that has begun.

Like it was said at Cole's funeral, we have to allow things like this to change our lives so we don't look back a few months later and see ourselves back in the ways we were in before. We pray that God will continue working in all the hearts that have been touched by His blessing of sending Cole to this earth with his special mission.

In following your journey the last few months, some things have been opened to me. One is the importance of lifting those in need of prayer to our Heavenly Father (sharing the burden). In this life the things that often seem important really are not... jobs, money, popularity, education, etc. What really DOES matter is that we love and care for others, trust God, be true lights in the world, and consider eternal things rather than the temporary.

Another is to love and cherish the children and look at their simple examples. The Bible says that children are the greatest in the kingdom of Heaven and that we are to become as little children. Their simple but true trust and faith in God surely does give strength for every day and every trial.

A third area is to trust God that His will may be done in all things, even when His will may not be our wants. We should know that God has a perfect plan for each and every one of us. This does not mean that we will not have trials, but we should ask God for understanding because He knows best.

We are continuing to pray for you and remembering the things that REALLY matter on our short journey through this life.

PSALM 46

1. GOD is our refuge and strength, a very present help in trouble.

2. Therefore will not we fear, though the earth be removed, and though the mountains be carried into the midst of the sea.

3. Though the waters thereof roar and be troubled, though the mountains shake with the swelling thereof. Selah.

4. There is a river, the streams whereof shall make glad the city of God, the holy place of the tabernacles of the most High.

5. God is in the midst of her; she shall not be moved: God shall help her, and that right early.

6. The heathen raged, the kingdoms were moved: he uttered his voice, the earth melted.

7. The Lord of hosts is with us; the God of Jacob is our refuge. Selah.

8. Come, behold the works of the Lord, what desolations he hath made in the earth.

9. He maketh wars to cease unto the end of the earth; he breaketh the bow, and cutteth the spear in sunder; he burneth the chariot in the fire.

10. Be still, and know that I am God: I will be exalted among the heathen, I will be exalted in the earth.

11. The Lord of hosts is with us; the God of Jacob is our refuge. Selah.

— From New Hampshire

* * * * * * *

Hi, Aaron and Moireen,

I just wanted to drop a note and say "hi" and let you know I was thinking of you and your family. The pictures of

Chaneille on CaringBridge are just adorable. Not a day goes by that I don't think of you and Cole. Your little man was just an angel of God. I have a feeling you will see a lot of Cole in the new baby. I'm not saying physically, but with actions. I think you will see Cole coming through in the new baby as a way of letting you know he's still with you. I'm sure he misses his baby sister too and watches over her sleep every night. May God continue to "Bless You" and your family.

I wish I could have been there with you at Cole's service, but at the same time, I don't know if I would have been able to hold up as well as you did. Just thinking about him makes me tear up.

Even though we have never met, you and your family have a spot in my heart. Cole has taught me to be kinder with my kids, not yell at them as much, and let them enjoy that extra piece of candy if it makes them happy. The kids got home from school today and the first thing I did was offer them a cup with ice cream (that was definitely a first from me). Their eyes lit up. Everyday I will make sure to do something special for them. I will make sure I wake them up with a kiss and put them to bed with a kiss and to love them "to the moon and back."

Cole has also brought me closer to God. I am actually reading the Bible and learning a lot from it. I thank God for bringing Cole into my life (even if it was just for a small period of time). But his love and memories will be with me for the rest of my life. Please continue to update your site as I want to always hear from you.

Love in Christ.

– From Texas

* * * * * * *

211

Dear Aaron and Moireen,

I have been thinking about you a lot and wanted to share one of my favorite memories of Cole. It was the weekend when Naomi and I were taking care of all the little cousins (except for Landen). I was downstairs with Cole and Chaneille and woke up to the sound of something dragging on the floor. I quickly got up and went to see what they were doing. I walked into the room and saw Chaneille in her crib with a bunch of toys around her with Cole sitting on his bed watching her. I asked him what they were doing. He told me that he didn't want Chaneille to cry and wanted to play with her. He had brought all those toys in for Chaneille to make her happy. He also helped me put all of them away. He was such a sweet big brother; he never cried when we put him to bed and was so kind to "his Chaneille."

Cole will be in my heart forever and in my mind very often. I miss him, but I'm so glad that Cole has no more pain and is in such a wonderful place! The last time I saw Cole was very special to me also. I got to hold his hand, hold his tiny feet, give him a kiss, and tell him that I loved him. I will always remember that!! I miss Cole so very much and am so honored that I was able to take care of him and play with him. Thank you for giving me the joy of doing that.

Cole has taught me that we shouldn't take life for granted, to enjoy the gifts God has given us each day, and to tell my family that I love them more, hug them more, and know that this is just our temporary home. Heaven is our real home!! I can't wait until I see Cole again. I will never forget Cole. I love you guys.

– From Michigan

* * * * * * *

I don't know where to even begin. For some reason when I found Cole's website I was drawn to it. I thought (and still do) about him and all of you all the time. I couldn't sleep anymore. I had to pray for Cole and his family.

I believe in God but didn't put my whole life in that realm of life (if that makes any sense at all). I have two children of my own and one stepchild. As you may have guessed, I am very busy, working full time and trying to be there for my children. My youngest is very much a handful (and to make a long story short, he has a lot of problems that we are just starting to figure out). He has been diagnosed with ADHD (attention-deficit hyperactivity disorder), and we are still working on the other part. He is out of control and has lots of "mishaps" (being unruly mostly) at school. He is a sweet 6-year-old with blond hair and blue eyes. He has a big heart, but is very troubled.

For a while I was feeling like I was over the edge and just couldn't take anymore. Then I found you all! I have a renewed breath now... You have helped me realize that I can still help him. My son (Konnor) and I have talked about Cole, and we've talked about your family and about Jesus. I feel like now we can conquer some goals set out there and "BE THERE."

Thank you for listening to me. Cole and your family will always be in my heart and in my prayers. If you are ever down in Kalamazoo, you should look us up. I'd be honored to meet you and your family.

– From Michigan

* * * * * * *

One of my favorite memories of Cole was during GKGW. He, Aiden, and I had these yellow foam balls that we called our "treasure." Josh (my younger brother) wanted to steal it so Cole, Aiden, and I hid it under chairs to protect it. All of a sudden, Josh turned into a "lion" and started growling and coming toward us. The boys started laughing and ran behind me, but I pretended to be terrified and started backing away, and I begged Cole and Aiden to protect me from this "terrifying beast."

At first, they were timid, but then Cole came from behind me and started to roar and growl. Josh acted as if he was scared. Cole giggled and looked at me with sparkling eyes as if to say "we got him now!" Aiden followed suit and started to scare the "beast." They scared that lion away from our "treasure" and saved me from a horrible fate. I then fainted in relief and fell to the floor. My rescuers laughed, tickled me, and kissed my face to wake me up.

I miss Cole terribly and will always think of him with a smile and a few tears. But I rejoice that he doesn't have to deal with this world anymore. We are aliens here; our real home is where Cole is – in HEAVEN with his Creator! Cole has taught me to live every moment with eternity in view, knowing that each day is a gift. I tell my family I love them and hug them a little longer. I won't forget Cole – I won't forget... I love you.

– From Michigan

I just wanted to say that following along with Cole's journey has changed my life forever. I have two sons that I have always adored more than anything. My husband and I work full-time jobs, so it was easy for us to take the little things for granted. Cole has taught me to spend more time with my family even though I am tired or stressed from work. I put those feelings on the back burner and try to realize what is most important to me... my family. I have also introduced God to my 2-year-old son Riley, which is something that I have never talked to him about in the past.

We say our prayers every night when I put him to bed, and when we are finished, he ALWAYS says Cole's name. I told him that Cole is an angel, so I think that really made an impression in his mind. I am Catholic, but I haven't been to church in a very long time. And to be honest, before Cole, I really didn't pray very often either. It was just another part of me that got caught up with the everyday stresses in life. Since getting to know Cole and the Ruotsala family through CaringBridge, I feel as though I have become a better person. Thank you so much.

Aaron, you are an amazing person. Good luck with your book.

(State name not given)

* * * * * * *

Aaron,

Cole taught me life is too short to be separated by our denominations. He also showed me that people are more precious than things.

(State name not given)

* * * * * * *

My life is forever changed by a little boy named Cole. Although I never met him, I knew of him through the CaringBridge website. Cole's journey has brought me closer to my children. I hold them a little tighter and appreciate the "small stuff" more. More importantly, Cole brought me closer to God... for that I am eternally grateful.

(State name not given)

* * * * * * *

Hi Aaron,

After reading your AWESOME entries to Caring- Bridge, I cannot help but comment and give a short (key word – I never write a short entry) testimonial about your precious son.

The very first time I saw a picture of Cole, it just hit me, as his being the total picture of the purity and innocence of a Christian and a child... to give me (and everyone else who saw him) the peace and comfort to be a faithful follower. I am not sure if it was in his eyes, smile, or what it was. Checking in on him just became an addiction.

Although I ALWAYS considered myself to be a Christian woman and a "believer," it was not until I "met" your son that I began to "write" and think like one... at the young and tender age of 39 years (NOT 40 YET!). It has not been something that I can say I am proud of that it took "this long" to really become a stronger person in faith. And it is a bit humbling to have it come from: A) a child; and B) someone I have never met on this side. It makes me wonder... WHY DID IT TAKE SO LONG???

I am the mother of three wonderful, adoring children, one (the oldest) of whom fought a tough but short battle with a brain tumor. He won, and I don't mean that he got his wings. He has been N.E.D. (no evidence of disease) since before starting the four hard rounds of chemo (Nov. 2007 through Mar. 2008), and getting ready for his 6-month post-treatment scans that are scheduled on Oct. 10. It makes me walk a little taller and appreciate each day that I wake up to see the sun a little brighter.

I hope this gives you some insight to the way Cole and your whole family has touched MY life.

With love and prayers.

– From Pennsylvania

Honoring Cole has become a mission in my daily life. When faced with situations throughout my day, I think of Cole and am reminded of the spirit of a beautiful little boy who taught me that with the love of family, of faith in God, and the ability to teach others through my actions. The time that we are granted on this earth should be spent honoring and serving God and never be taken for granted. Cole was truly an angel sent to us all with a purpose far greater than we understood throughout his journey with us! Until I meet you, sweet angel boy, thank you for teaching me the greatest lessons of my life – I love you to the moon and back, Cole.

(State name not given)

* * * * * * *

Your family is truly a blessing!!! Wow! God truly has a purpose for all of us, no matter what our age. Cole's passing taught us to be more appreciative for what we have this very moment for it may not last long, but the memories will last a lifetime, which is a great gift in itself. Thank you for sharing your story and keeping such a strong faith throughout. We are supposed to share God's Word, and what a wonderful job you have all done!

What happened to your family could have happened to anyone of us, but I believe Cole was chosen because he left the largest imprint on so many hearts. He was an angel who served God and completed his purpose like no one else could. He will never be forgotten! God Bless!

– From South Dakota

* * * * * * *

Editor's Note:
Only minor changes have been made to the Guestbook letters in order to retain the writer's integrity,

LaVergne, TN USA
05 November 2010
203689LV00002B/1/P